From Sa
to Speed

A NEW HISTORY OF OLD
BEDFORD

Ian Freeman

The
Book
Castle

First published November 2006
by
The Book Castle
12 Church Street
Dunstable
Bedfordshire LU5 4RU

ISBN 1 903747 73 2
ISBN 978 1 903747 73 5

Typeset and designed by Caroline and Roger Hillier
The Old Chapel Graphic Design
www.theoldchapelivinghoe.com

Printed in Great Britain by TJ International Ltd, Padstow, Cornwall

"Much of that which is called local history is, unhappily, of very questionable origin, but, having been once published, is accepted without suspicion, and copied by all subsequent careless compilers. In this way great errors are handed down, and it is astonishing how pertinaciously some writers will help to perpetuate even positive blunders which a little research on their own part might have corrected".

James Wyatt
Beds. Architectural and Archaeological Society Volume II p 256

About the Author

Although Dr Freeman was a food chemist by profession, he has always been interested in local history. He first became actively interested in researching the subject when he was living in Hertfordshire. He was a founder member of the Harpenden Local History Society and made several contributions to Herts. Arch. Review and to Hertfordshire's Past. On moving to Bedford, he transferred his interest to the history of that county and joined The Bedford Archaeological Society (now the Bedford Arch. and Local History Society). He served as president of that Society for many years. He has made several contributions to the now defunct Bedfordshire Magazine and to Bedfordshire Archaeology.

Acknowledgements

This book started as a project by a team of members of The Bedfordshire Archaeological Society. In the beginning the project had the limited object of explaining the origins of Bedford street names. The team consisted of Mr Arthur Guppy, Mr Alan Crawley and myself.

Sadly, Mr Guppy died while the project was still in its early stages and Mr Crawley had to drop out later, due to ill health. Although the project eventually expanded to cover the early history of Bedford Town in general, the work of Mr Guppy and Mr Crawley were valuable contributions to that final form.

I must also thank Miss Patricia Bell and Mr James Collet-White for useful discussions and guidance through the archives of the Bedford County Record Office. I would also like to thank Mr Lionel Mumby — one-time tutor in Local History Studies at Cambridge Further Education Department, Madingley — for teaching me that local history did not necessarily have to be only a spectator sport but that amateurs could make a useful contribution.

Finally, I have to thank my wife for her patience and tolerance when the book was occupying a lot of my time and was causing me to hog the family typewriter and the dining room table.

Contents

Sources

Most of the early material is taken from *The Anglo-Saxon Chronicles*, together with *Asser's Life of King Alfred* as transcribed by Simon Keynes and Michael Lapidge in the Penguin Classic, *Alfred the Great* (1983). Other early material can be found in *English Historical Documents Vol. 1*. Aethelgifu's will has been transcribed and translated by Dorothy Whitelock for the Roxburghe Club, Oxford 1968.

For the Medieval period, much use has been made of the publications of the Bedford Historical Record Society, especially *Vol XLIII, Newnham Cartulary*, *Vol XXV, Newnham Priory Rental* and *Vol XXXVI, The Black Book of Bedford*. Matthew Paris' writings, *Chronica Majora* and *Gesta Monasterii Sancta Albani*, can be found in the Rolls Series.

A very full account of the affair of Philip de Brois and the consequent schism between Henry II and Thomas Becket can be found in *Becket* by Richard Winter (Constable 1967).

Further details about street names can be found in two articles by I.P. Freeman and A. Crawley in Vols. 18 and 19 of *Bedford Archaeology*. Articles on individual streets were published by the same authors in the now defunct *Bedfordshire Magazine* at frequent but irregular intervals during the years 1989 to 1997.

Early deeds and charters relating to specific sites in the town are kept in the County Record Office, (Bedford and Luton Archives and Records Services).

Introduction

No comprehensive history of Bedford town has been published since Joyce Godber's "The Story of Bedford" in 1978. This book is a new attempt to write at least a part of that story. It is new in the sense that I have tried to follow the warning issued by James Wyatt which I have quoted earlier. That is, I have endeavoured to consult, whenever possible, primary sources and early chronicles and, where I have had to rely on later authors, I have made it clear that I have done so.

Following this maxim, I have uncovered several facts which have not been reported in earlier histories and so corrected several previously published items which have proved to be based on false or insufficient evidence.

This history is also new in that it concentrates on the early history of Bedford town. This has been treated in a somewhat perfunctory way by previous authors, mainly because information from "The Dark Ages" takes some digging out while an abundance of information from later centuries comes readily to hand.

Because of the sparsity of firm information on this early period, I have resorted to some speculation to fill the gaps. I believe those speculations are feasible interpolations from established knowledge and I hope they will be taken up by later historians who will prove them to be not too far off the mark or else refute them. Either way, some of the gaps in our knowledge may be filled.

The first part of the book covers the period from early Saxon times, when Bedford was emerging from the mists of speculative history, through the time of King Offa, when speculation is based on some historical facts off and on to the reign of King Alfred, when Bedford's name was first firmly fixed in recorded history. The second part covers the Norman and later medieval periods, outlining the events and institutions which shaped the town of Bedford at that time. The third part takes a look in some detail at the town as depicted in John Speed's map published in 1610. This map is the first street map of Bedford town and was published at the time when Bedford was still largely confined within its early boundaries and street plan just before it began to expand to become the town it is today. It is therefore a useful pivotal point. This part of the book looks in detail at the town to examine what remains of that street plan and to discuss some of the town's more notable inhabitants and the places where they lived. Some of those buildings have survived but many have been lost as a result of Bedford's many attempts to improve itself.

PART ONE

Saxon
Bedford

up to 11th century

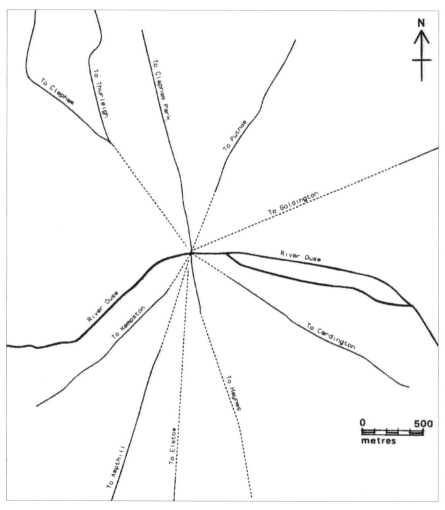

above Alignment of roads approaching Bedford onto the river crossing.

right Channel of River Ouse as it goes through Bedford showing the river crossing

at the narrowest point.

Chapter I

Geographical Significance
of Bedford

When looking into the origins of any settlement the first question one must ask is why the settlement came to be established where it was. In the case of Bedford, the answer lies in the name. The earliest settlement at 'Bedford', i.e. Beda's Ford, must have grown up around a river crossing. The geology of the area shows that the ford was at a point where the channel of the River Ouse was at its narrowest for several miles up or down stream. We will probably never know who Beda was, but we can deduce that his ford was of more importance than many other local fords because of the effect it had on the pattern of the roads approaching it.

An examination of the Ordnance Survey map for the area around Bedford shows that most of the roads heading towards the town align on a single point on the river, approximating to the present position of the Town Bridge. The roads, before the

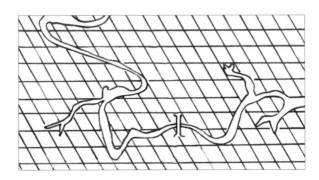

settlement became a town, radiated from the river crossing like the spokes of a spider's web. Only one of these has survived to reach and indeed to cross the river without deflection from its original line. This line started from Clapham and followed the footpath which now takes it down to Brickhill Drive. After crossing that road, it follows the footpath along the western edge of the old cemetery and then becomes the modern Foster Hill Road. In the Middle Ages this was known as Clapham Park Way. It was named Foster Hill Road after the Foster family who at one time owned Brickhill Farm, whose homestead once stood near the shops in Brickhill Drive.

The line of Foster Hill Road is continued right through the town along the High Street, although the connection has become obscured by the development of De Parys Avenue. The road continued over the bridge and along St Mary's Street and St John's Street. There is some evidence, in the form of footpaths and minor roads, that it continued in the direction of Haynes.

All the other radial roads were deflected from their direct connections with the river crossing when the Saxon burh, which was the precursor to the medieval town, was constructed. The approach from the north east was along the southern end of what is now Kimbolton Road. Near the end of what is now Ellis Road, this road split into three. One branch continued along the present Kimbolton Road for about half a mile then turned west along a little lane which later developed into Falcon Avenue. This lane at one time marked the boundary between the borough of Bedford with Putnoe/Goldington. This explains the wide hedgerow which runs down the middle of Falcon Avenue. Another line branched off along what is now Putnoe Lane. (The present Putnoe Lane has been deflected slightly at its southern end to make a square junction with Kimbolton Road, but originally it branched off at an acute angle). The third road has now disappeared under the expansion of modern Bedford. This bisected the angle between the other two roads, lying slightly to the east of the present Kimbolton Road. An estate map of 1774 clearly shows these three roads. The copy held in the Record Office has a line added to it sometime after the map had first been drawn. This marks the line of the present Kimbolton Road and was presumably added to the map during the planning stage of the Kimbolton Turnpike, construction of which started in 1795. The added line follows, initially, the line of the most westerly of the three diverging roads but ignores the turn down Falcon Avenue and picks up the line of the middle road at a point some 1,000 yards from the point of divergence. This was an example of the practice used to construct the turnpike, all the way to Kimbolton; existing lanes were picked up and developed, where appropriate, and these were linked by relatively straight stretches of new road.

From the O.S. map it is obvious that this originally led down to the river crossing, but it now takes a sharp turn to the west along St Peter's Street, following a line which, as we shall see later, runs just outside the northern boundary of the old town, and eventually entering the town through its northern gateway.

The approach road from the east came from Goldington. The old alignment on the river crossing can be picked up just west of Goldington Green, but between there and Bedford the old road has undergone a number of changes. The first deflection, resulting from the construction of the northern Saxon burh, took it across the Rothsay area along Newnham Street to enter the burh near St Cuthbert's Church. It then followed Mill Street to the central crossroads of the burh where it intersects with the High Street. Later the road from Goldington forked into two Goldington Roads, the one leading to the central crossroads while the other diverged from this to follow a more northerly line across the present Goldington Road to join the Kimbolton Road at its junction with St. Peter's Street. In the eighteenth century, these two roads co-existed and were known respectively as Little Goldington Highway and Great Goldington Highway.

On the north western side of the town was a road which is now almost completely lost, the Thurleigh Way. This started from Scauld End in Thurleigh and traversed the countryside to Manton Heights. It eventually came along what is now a rear access road called Slade Walk, before joining Clapham Road. The Thurleigh Way can now only be picked out from old maps such as the Clapham Tithe map and appears on the ground only as old farm tracks and hedgerows. Where it merges with the Clapham Road, the latter is deflected to the south and the combined roads are aligned on the river crossing. This deflection of the Clapham Road is still apparent in the modern road although somewhat obscured by the roundabout at the end of Union Street. The route taken by the road when deflected by the burh is not clear. It might have followed the present Tavistock Street to enter the burh at its northern entrance near St Peter's Church or it might have followed along what is now Union Street and Dame Alice Street to the same northern entrance. Cary's map of 1801 shows the main route out to Clapham along Union Street, while a sketch plan of 1750 shows Dame Alice Street as "back lane that leads to Clapham". Also, both Cary's map and Jeffery's map of 1765 show Tavistock Street as not leading to Clapham. On the other hand, there are field boundaries running across Dame Alice Street which imply that the street was a late development.

This is certainly the case with the Bromham Road which is a continuation of Dame Alice Street. Not only does it by-pass the village centres of both Biddenham and Bromham but it also cuts across the pattern of open fields on the western side of the town, showing that it post-dated those fields. Bromham Bridge was originally called Biddenham Bridge and there is some evidence that the road was approached by a road leading directly from Biddenham village. The pattern of roads through Biddenham supports that suggestion but it also suggests a possible river crossing immediately west of Biddenham Church. Before the Bromham Road was constructed, Biddenham would have been approached from Bedford along what is now Midland Road and Ford End Road. That road was respected by the open field pattern.

South of the river, Cauldwell Street and Cardington Road both show obvious alignments on the river crossing, although both are now deflected to the crossroads near St Mary's Church. The Ampthill Road is also aligned on the river crossing but is now deflected to the southern entrance to the town near St John's Church. Elstow Road also shows an alignment on the crossing, but as it approaches the town it has undergone a number of diversions before joining the Ampthill Road just outside the southern entrance to the town. One such diversion took place in 1305 when the road was re-routed to go round St. Leonard's Hospital (see below).

Although the alignment of the roads onto the crossing is apparent on the map, it is not, in most cases, visible on the ground. This is because the roads were deflected from their original course by development of the town. There are, however, two points from which the alignment can still be seen quite clearly. One of these is on the road from Clapham Park.

If one stands on the footpath alongside the cemetery, one can look straight down Foster Hill Road and see, in direct line, the high rise block which is the Moat House Hotel. This stands adjacent to the bridge and so serves as a useful marker demonstrating, quite clearly, the alignment on the river crossing.

The hotel also serves as a useful alignment point for the road

View looking south down Foster Hill Road, showing how it is aligned
on the river crossing (indicated by the Moat House Hotel.).

View looking east along Cauldwell Street showing how it is aligned directly on the river crossing (as shown by the Moat House Hotel) before it veers to the right towards St Mary's Church).

from Kempston, i.e. Cauldwell Street.

One can stand at a point near County Hall and see the hotel at the end of the alignment, although the present road veers to the right before it reaches that point.

It is obvious from those alignments why Beda's Ford should have been considered so important and that it was almost inevitable some form of settlement would have formed there. Nothing is known about this early settlement. Archaeology has uncovered much evidence of earlier occupation in the surrounding area, including material from Bronze Age, Iron Age, the Roman period and an early Saxon cemetery at Kempston, just outside Bedford. But, in the town itself, so far nothing has been revealed which pre-dates the 9th century. So the oldest feature of Bedford town is in fact its name. Some historians have argued that an early form of the name is Biedcanford and associate it with the battle which took place at that site. This is reported in the Anglo-Saxon Chronicle for the year 571. "Cuthwulf fought the Brito-Welsh at Biedcanford and took four villages — Limbury, Aylesbury, Bensington and Eynsham".

These places can all be identified with modern places which lie on a line along the Icknield Way and westward. So it is tempting to postulate that Cuthwulf forced a bridgehead at what is now Bedford and was then in a position to advance through the other places. However, place name experts are unanimous in the view that "Biedcanford" would not evolve into "Bedford". So unless and until some strong evidence of an anomalous change can be demonstrated, the identification of Bedford with Biedcanford has to be rejected.

Position of Bedford in relation to those towns mentioned in the Anglo-Saxon Chronicle entry for 571 A.D.

King Offa, supervising the excavation of St Alban's grave – from a sketch by Matthew Paris.

Chapter 2

King Offa and Bedford

Some two centuries later than the Battle of Biedcanford, Bedford begins to emerge from the mists of conjecture onto firmer ground. In the year 796, King Offa, the great Mercian king, died. It is generally accepted that he was the founder of St Alban's Abbey, and the monks of the Abbey have chronicled his death and his burial. Matthew Paris, writing in the 13th century, gives us the fullest account in his Chronica Majora: "In that year (796) Offa, the great king of the Mercians, having nearly constructed a most noble monastery following the discovery of the blessed Alban, met his end in the town called Offley according to the opinion of many – (Offley is now Great Offley in Hertfordshire) – whose body was said to be buried with regal ceremony near the town of Bedford in a chapel outside the town sited on the banks of the River Ouse. However, it is related to this day by nearly all the people of the area, that the said chapel due to long wear and the violence of that river, was broken down and together with the royal tomb was swept down into the river; from then up to the present, the tomb has been diligently sought by the men of the place, when bathing in the summer time and whenever the depth of the water is visible and whenever possible and as if it were a thing destined, has not been discovered".

Matthew Paris uses phrases like "in the opinion of many" and "it is related by nearly all the people of the area", so he appears to be slightly sceptical of the story himself. However, as he shows in his other great work, "Gesta Abbatum Monasterii Sancta Albani", he was sufficiently convinced to berate two Abbots of St Albans for not taking greater care of Offa's body. The first of these was Abbot Willegod who died in 796, the same year as King Offa, so it is perhaps a little unfair of Matthew to criticise him in this way. The other abbot, though, was Paul who was in office from 1077 to 1093, i.e. some three centuries after Offa's death. The fact that he was open to an accusation of neglecting Offa's tomb indicates that it must have been in situ during his lifetime and that disaster struck the royal tomb at least two centuries after it was first set up. Willegod was Abbot at the time the Saxon abbey was being built and Paul, as the first Norman abbot, was in office at the time the Norman abbey, i.e. the great church we can see today, was under construction. So both these men would have been in a position to incorporate Offa's tomb in their plans for the new buildings. This, no doubt, was why Matthew Paris picked these two men out for criticism.

We must remember that Matthew Paris was writing some 150 years after Paul's term of office, so his account can hardly be taken as contemporary even assuming that, as official chronicler to the Abbey, he would have access to records of the time. However, some support is lent to the story by the fact that no other place has made a sustainable claim to be the site of Offa's tomb, although there are several places which one might consider to be more likely. These include St. Alban's Abbey itself but also Lichfield, which was the seat of the Archbishopric of Mercia which Offa set up in 787, and Repton, where other important Mercian kings were buried.

One author has made the statement that Queen Cynethryth, the widow of King Offa, "ended her days as Abbess of Bedford". However, the evidence presented by the author is not conclusive. It derives from an account of the proceedings at a synod of "Clofesho" held in 798, significantly, perhaps, only two years after Offa's death. The main item on the agenda concerned a long standing claim which the Archbishop of Canterbury had to a monastery at Cookham. It appears that the lands at Cookham had been granted to Archbishop Cuthbert of Canterbury by Aethelbald, king of Mercia at the time. However, the deeds were stolen and given to Cynewulf, king of the West Saxons. When Offa annexed the land around Cookham and took it into Mercia, he retained the monastery and its lands for as long as he lived and left it to his heirs "without evidence of documents", such that after their deaths the lands should be consigned to the church which is situated at Bedeford(sic). The dispute was resolved by an arrangement whereby Abbess Cynethryth of Cookham (i.e. of the same name as Offa's widow) should retain the lands and the monastery at Cookham but cede lands in Kent to Canterbury.

A transcription of the proceedings at Clofesho can be found in English Historical Documents vol. I item 79. On the face of it, it does suggest that Queen Cynethryth had become an Abbess and that she had connections with the church at Bedford. However, in her commentary Dorothy Whitelock makes the point that "Bedeford" cannot be identified with Bedford nor can Abbess Cynethryth be identified with certainty with Queen Cynethryth. Margaret Gelling has also pointed out that, although Bedeford is a later form of Bedford, it was not the current form at the time of the synod. There is evidence for an abbey at Bedford but that is not till nearly two centuries later.

Whatever the truth of these various points, it is inconceivable that Offa would be unaware of the strategic importance of this crossing over one of the major rivers of his kingdom. It has been suggested that Bedford was in fact part of a defensive system set up by Offa with Viking incursions in mind. This would have involved a series of fortifications placed to block the main rivers penetrating into Mercia. The triple obligation of service in a defence force, maintenance of fortresses and maintenance of bridges had been established by the time of Offa's reign, so it is reasonable to surmise that the ford was replaced by a bridge as part of Offa's plan. This would not justify, though, the assumption that Offa was also responsible for the rectilinear pattern of streets that formed the nucleus of the old town and which can still be picked out among the modern streets.

A much stronger case can be made out for attributing this pattern to a later and greater Saxon king.

King Alfred the Great, as portrayed on a coin of his reign.

Chapter 3

King Alfred and Bedford

It was not until the reign of King Alfred that the name Bedford takes its place incontestably, in English history.

During the 9th century, Viking commando raids around the coasts of England had developed into a full scale invasion. The Danish forces had conquered East Anglia, Northumbria and Mercia and were well on the way to subjugating Wessex. Alfred, King of Wessex, was reduced to defending Wessex by a strategy of guerrilla warfare. Eventually, though, with the help of his allies, Alfred was able to assemble an army strong enough to confront the Danes in open battle. The battle took place at Ethandun (alias Edington) in the year 878. The Danish force, under Guthrum, was defeated and Guthrum acknowledged Alfred's victory by submitting to Christian baptism under the sponsorship of Alfred. He then withdrew into East Anglia to consolidate a Danish kingdom there. The war against other Danish forces continued, however, and it was only after "Many towns had been burnt and so many people slaughtered" that Alfred was able to occupy London and all the Angles and Saxons — those who had formerly been scattered everywhere and were not in captivity with the Vikings — turned willingly to King Alfred and submitted themselves to his lordship.

London had been a Mercian city before the Danish occupation and Alfred wisely chose a Mercian, Ethelred the Elderman, to rebuild its defences. He did this by, in effect, constructing a new burh between the old Roman city to the east and the earlier Saxon settlement of Lundewic to the west. This had the rectangular

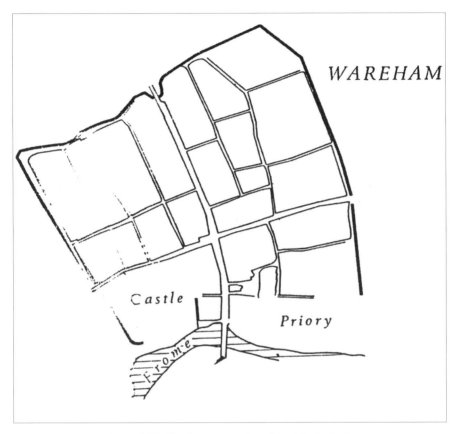

above and right Rectilinear street plans of two Alfredian burhs.

street plan which has come to be recognised as the hallmark
of an Alfredian burh. These burhs were constructed as part of
Alfred's defence plan against the Danes. They were townships in
which people lived and worked, but surrounded by a defensive
boundary and with their streets laid out on a standard rectilinear
pattern. This arrangement can still be seen, for instance, in such
well known Alfredian burhs as Wareham and Wallingford. The
resemblance between the street plans of these towns and that
of Bedford cannot be ignored. The pattern is very obvious in

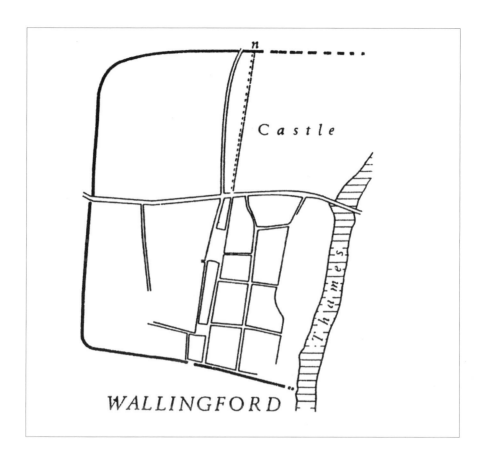

John Speed's map of Bedford town. This was published in 1610, before Bedford had started to expand, so it is a unique snapshot of the old town.

Although it was situated in Mercia rather than in Alfred's Wessex, it is not difficult to trace out a sequence of events which would bring Bedford into Alfred's defence scheme and explain how it came to be an Alfredian burh.

London had been liberated in the year 886. Sometime between then and the year of Guthrum's death in 890, Alfred and Guthrum attempted to stabilise the situation by agreeing to the division of the country between English and Danish territories. The terms of the agreement are set out in a treaty known variously as the treaty of Wedmore or the treaty of Chippenham. This defined a boundary line which started from the Thames, up the River Lea to its source, then in a straight line north to Bedford, along the River Ouse to Watling Street and so on to the North West. For the most part, this follows a simple NW to SE diagonal line along well-defined topographical features i.e. the rivers and the Roman road. But there is one very significant diversion from that simple design. Instead of taking the line directly from the source of the Lea, i.e. at Leagrave, across to Watling Street at some point near Houghton Regis, a gap of about 5 kilometres, the line was deflected north, some 30 kilometres, across country with no obvious topographical features, to take in Bedford. This is clearly a deliberate decision to include Bedford in the treaty boundary. It is the only town to be mentioned in the treaty document. This implies that Alfred was determined to keep Bedford under Saxon control. We have seen how important strategically this river crossing was. The second part of the treaty shows that Alfred was in a strong enough position to insist on this. It laid down rules governing the status of Englishmen and Danes on both sides of the boundary. Thus the treaty left Bedford under Saxon control.

Near the Guildhall in London there is an area known as The Aldermanbury which means "Elderman's Fortified Residence". This is generally accepted as marking the residence of Ethelred of Mercia and commemorates his part in the re-fortification of London. Bedford also had a district of Aldermanbury but the name has not been found in any other town, though all Saxon towns must, at one time or another, have come under the jurisdiction of an elderman. It is reasonable to suppose then that

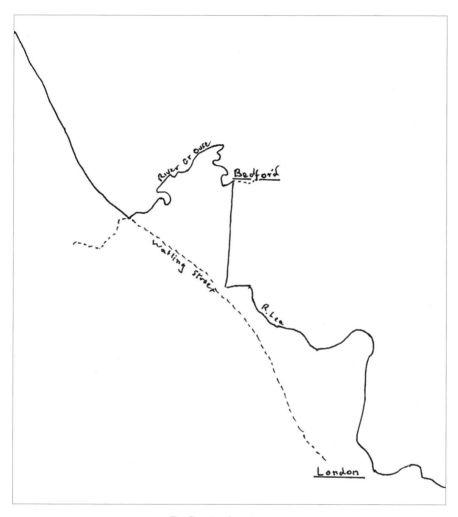

The Danelaw Boundary.

Ethelred was involved in the fortification of Bedford just as he was in the fortification of London and that it was he who set up the rectilinear street grid just as he had in London.

The Danelaw boundary, as it came to be called, ran across the old kingdom of Mercia, separating an English half from a Danish half. Alfred could have chosen to annex the English half into an expanded Wessex. Instead, he took the wiser course and gave the Angles of Mercia some degree of autonomy by appointing Ethelred as Viceroy, or Subregulus as he is described in some charters. He also cemented his personal relationship with Ethelred by allowing him to marry his daughter, Ethelfreda, who came to be known as the Lady of the Mercians. Together the couple were to campaign against the Danes to the northwest, building burhs at Warwick and Worcester which reflect the rectilinear plan.

A document known as the Burghal Hideage lays down guidelines for the garrisoning of the burhs. This lists a number of places to which the guidelines applied. Bedford does not appear in the list; most of the towns that do were in Wessex, but Bedford fits in well with the specifications laid down. According to these, every pole of defence perimeter was to have four men to defend it and every man was to have back-up support of one hide of land. The perimeter of the burh of Bedford has been estimated at between 250 and 350 poles. This would require between 1,000 and 1,400 men to defend it, with a back-up of 1,000 to 1,400 hides of land. The Domesday Book, was later to assess the County of Bedford at 1,200 hides, well within that bracket.

Thus Bedford had all the characteristics of an Alfredian burh and its creation as such is not only compatible with the known history of the time but also explains an otherwise unexplained anomaly in the line of the Danelaw Boundary.

Although the Danelaw survived as a legal concept until well into the Norman period, the boundary itself did not survive very long as a treaty demarcation line. After only a few years, the Danes pushed south and west and reoccupied Bedford and other parts of the county. The town was then to remain in Danish hands until Edward the Elder, Alfred's son and successor, began his campaign to push the Danes back north.

The Anglo-Saxon Chronicles tell us that, in the year 914 "before Martinmas, King Edward went to Buckingham with his troops, stayed there four weeks, and built the strongholds on either side of the river before he left. Earl Thurcytel sought him there for his lord and all the eorls and most senior men who belonged to Bedford; also many who belonged to Northampton". The Chronicles go on to say that in 915 "King Edward went with troops to Bedford before Martinmass, got possession of the burh and most of the town dwellers that had been living there turned to him. He stayed there four weeks, and commanded the burh to be built on the south side of the river before he went from there". In the following year, 916, the Chronicles tell us that Thurcytel, who had been the Danish commander at Bedford, "went over the sea to Frankland with those men who would serve him, with King Edward's peace and help".

Tradition has it that the King's Ditch marked the boundary of the burh south of the river. This Ditch, of which only fragments have survived, until relatively recently formed a D-shaped earthwork, enclosing a large area on the south of the river. Despite the traditional belief, there is no archaeological evidence to support the idea that it dates from King Edward's time. The first known author to mention the idea was Camden, writing as late as the 16th century. The earliest remains found, so far, date from the Norman period. Furthermore a burh of the size enclosed by the ditch would make little strategic sense. The burh would be at least as large as the original burh on the north side of the river and the combined perimeter would require double the garrison. Edward built similar burhs on the south side of the rivers at Stamford and at Nottingham. No ditches have been found at those places. It is more likely that these burhs were of the

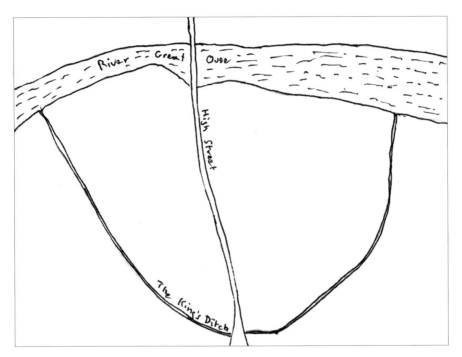

The King's Ditch.

type which he built at Witham in Essex in 913. This comprised an elliptical enclosure of about 400 yards by 350 yards against the eastern bank of the River Brain. Edwards's burhs, unlike Alfred's burhs, were not intended as defended towns but were purely military constructions to defend the bridgeheads at each town.

In 917, the Danes made another attempt on Bedford, advancing up the Ouse from Tempsford, but this was successfully beaten off. According to the Anglo-Saxon Chronicles, "At the same time, the force went out from Huntington and East Anglia, made the fort at Tempsford, lived there and built it up, and forsook the other at Huntingdon; they thought that from there they would be able to reach more land with strife and hostility.

They went until they arrived at Bedford; then the men that were inside came out, fought them, put them to flight and killed a good part of them". The Chronicle goes on to say, "After that summer, many folk under Edward's rule, and all the men from the nearest burhs who could reach it, went to Tempsford and besieged the town. They fought until they broke in and killed the king, eorl Toglos, eorl Manna his son, his brother and all who were inside who meant to defend it, and captured the others and everything that was within".

When Russell Park was being laid out at the end of the 19th century, some graves were uncovered. These were oriented east to west in the Christian tradition but they also contained weapons, so they were obviously the graves of warriors. Some of the weapons can be seen in Bedford Museum. It seems likely that these were the graves of those who fell during this defence of Bedford against the Danes.

After Edward's successful campaign, Bedford was not troubled by the Danes until 1010, during the disastrous reign of Ethelred the Unready when a Danish force swept through Buckingham and Bedford and on to Tempsford "ever burning where they went".

During the intervening century, Bedford featured only occasionally in the historical headlines. In the year 971, Oscytel, Archbishop of York died and his body was brought to Bedford by his kinsman, Abbot Thurcytel, "because he was abbot there at the time". (It is interesting to note that both "Oscytel" and "Thurcytel" are Danish names. "Thurcytel" is, in fact, the same name as that of the Danish commander who had surrendered to Edward in 915. How rapidly had the once pagan Danes integrated into the Christian establishment). One wonders, though, what sort of an establishment Thurcytel's abbey really was. Not long after the death of Oskytel a lady called Aethelgifu made a will leaving bequests to churches in Hertfordshire and Bedfordshire. These include "fifty sheep to Bedford". In her commentary on the will, Dorothy Whitelock suggested that the churches named were mostly minsters, i.e. central churches with a team of priests to cover a wide area of the surrounding countryside which was the system before the smaller parishes with one resident priest had developed. In a later period, St. Paul's Church in Bedford was run as a collegiate church with a team of irregular canons. This was, almost certainly, the minster which benefited from Aethelgifu's will. Could it also have been Thurcytel's "Abbey"?

PART TWO

Norman Bedford

11th to 16th centuries

Chapter 4

Norman Changes to the Town

After the relatively peaceful time at the end of the Saxon period, the face of England was radically changed by the Norman Conquest of 1066. Bedford did not escape. Very soon after the beginning of the occupation two radical changes to the topography of the town were made. About a quarter of the town north of the river was cleared to make room for the building of the castle and a new suburb was developed south of the river.

The Castle

A roughly square-shaped area was carved out of the town to make room for the castle. The southern boundary of this enclave was formed by the river. There was a ditch marking the western boundary, running parallel to the High Street and about 30m to the east of it. This turned to the east at what is now Luddington's Passage, formerly Ram Yard. The northern boundary finished just to the west of what is now Newnham Street. Here it turned south to follow the western side of that street, then back to the river to complete the square. The first castle would have been of the motte and bailey type, with a wooden tower, but at some time this was replaced by a stone keep. Today only the mound remains.

The Norman castles were originally built as a means of subjugating the Saxon population, but Bedford Castle, on three occasions, found itself on the defensive. The first of these was in 1137, during the civil war between Stephen and Matilda to decide who should hold the crown of England. Bedford Castle was at that time in the hands of Miles de Beauchamp, grandson of Hugh de Beauchamp who had acquired the castle at a very early stage in the Norman occupation and who is accredited with it in the Domesday Book. Stephen, wishing to ensure he had control of Bedford, called upon Miles to surrender the castle. Miles, although willing to recognise Stephen's claim to the throne, was reluctant to yield possession. This attitude did not satisfy Stephen and he laid siege to the castle. Frontal attack did not succeed but, after five weeks of siege, Miles was forced to surrender due to lack of supplies. Later, in 1141, when the tide of war had turned somewhat, Miles was able to re-occupy the castle. In 1153 though, there was another attack on the castle. This time the attackers were led by Prince Henry, the son of Matilda, later to become King Henry II. The Prince's forces heavily plundered the town and caused severe damage, especially to St. Paul's Church. However, he did have the grace to grant to the church £8 from the Bedford Hagable and a further grant of £2 "if this is practible" to make good the damage to the church.

The castle remained under the control of the Beauchamps for a further sixty years. However, in 1215, they once again got on the wrong side of the ruling king, when William de Beauchamp cast his lot with the barons who exacted Magna Carta from King John. His "reward" for this was to lose his castle which was taken from him on the King's instruction and given to the King's supporter, Faulkes de Breaute. According to the chronicler, Ralf de Coggeshall, "King John had a certain servant, faithful and daring, who was nicknamed Falco, from the scythe with which he had slain a soldier on his father's land in Normandy; to whom he first entrusted a ward on the Welsh marches, where with his friends and fellows, he had ravaged and massacred; so that from the lowest estate he had quickly become famous, capable and highly distinguished among those serving the king". Under the protection of John, Faulkes committed a number of atrocities mainly against churches. Among other things he harassed the abbeys of St. Albans and Warden demanding "protection money" from them. He demolished parts of the churches of St Paul and St Cuthbert in Bedford and used the stone to reinforce the defences of his castle; he annexed land from the Abbess of Elstow. When John died in 1216, and was succeeded by Henry III, Faulkes lost his royal protector. Henry was determined to bring Faulkes to book. In 1224 he sent a team of justices to Dunstable to investigate Faulkes' activities. Faulkes' response to this was to send his brother, William, to detain the justices. Two of the justices managed to escape but the third member of the team, Henry de Braibroc, was arrested and incarcerated in the castle at Bedford. Of course, King Henry could not tolerate this. He raised an army and laid siege to the castle. A detailed account of the siege has been compiled by A.R. Goddard in his book "The Great Siege of Bedford Castle". Resources and men were recruited for the king's army from all over the country and the army was equipped with state of the art artillery, such as mangonels and petraries to hurl great stones against the castle walls.

The castle fell after a siege lasting nine weeks. Henry had vowed that he would hang all those who had taken part in the defence of the castle. He fulfilled this vow to the letter. Faulkes himself escaped death as he was away at the time, but his brother, William, and many others were hanged in fulfilment of the King's vow. Three of these though, did not die. These were Knights Templar. Henry had them strung up to fulfil his vow but immediately had them cut down so that they survived to journey to the Holy Land. We do not know how these men came to be involved in the defence of the castle but Henry's leniency towards them illustrates the power which the Templars had at that time.

Following the siege, Henry ordered the castle to be razed to the ground. The site was returned to William de Beauchamp with the proviso that he could only build an unfortified house on it. There is no evidence that William built anything on the site and it passed out of Beauchamp hands when William's son, John, died at the battle of Evesham in 1265, while fighting alongside Simon de Montford; yet another Beauchamp who chose the wrong side in a dispute with his king. The castle estate then passed to Thomas de Mowbray through his marriage to one of John's daughters.

The siege was the last occasion when the castle was the centre of military activity although, for a short time, the mound was occupied by Parliamentary forces during the Civil War of the 17th century. Charles I started the war by raising his standard at Nottingham in August 1642. In Bedford, Parliament responded by issuing an authority for a fort to be set up on the castle mound. Some walls were constructed with loop holes for firing through and the fort was garrisoned with about 500 men. In subsequent years, there were troop movements through Bedford, both Parliamentary and Royalist, and there was some fighting on Bedford Bridge. But there is no record of any actual fighting at the fort. The fort was not popular with the inhabitants of Bedford. They saw it as attracting military activity to the town rather than defending it. There was a petition to Parliament to have the fort removed and, in 1645, it was dismantled by order of Parliament. After that, the castle mound has remained unoccupied to the present day. The only conflict it was to see was between sporting competitors when the flat top of the mound was used as a bowling green in the 18th century.

The Southern Town

The other major effect the Normans had on the appearance of Bedford town was the development of a new suburb on the south side of the river. This was bounded by the King's Ditch. This ditch is clearly shown on maps of the town up to relatively recent times but it is now almost completely covered in. Only a few stretches are still visible. One of these is a short length running across the traffic roundabout at the southern end of St John's Street. Other fragments can be seen behind St John's Hospital and in the grounds of Dame Alice School. It originally formed a rough semi-circle, with its western end leaving the River Ouse from the southern bank opposite Batt's Ford, passing through the still exposed stretch at the bottom of St John's Street, then turning north towards the river again to a point just below Duck Mill Weir. This most easterly point is marked by King's Ditch Bridge which carries the public footpath over the Ditch.

The earliest known reference to the Ditch by name is in a court case of 1330. At that time, the Ditch was 32ft in width at the top and 16ft at the bottom. The case was brought by the Justices of the County of Bedford against various people accused of filling in the Ditch "to the damage of the Lord the King and the peril of the aforesaid township". The accused included the Prior of Caldwell. As the property of the Priory was bounded on one side by the Ditch, there is little doubt that this was indeed the same ditch.

By tradition, the Ditch is associated with Edward the Elder who ordered a burh to be built on the south side of the river during the four weeks he was staying in Bedford after he had taken possession of the town from the Danes in 915. However, this tradition can only be traced back to William Camden writing in his "Britannia" as late as 1586. The unlikelihood of the Ditch being constructed by Edward is discussed above. No conclusive archaeological evidence for a 10th century origin for the Ditch has been uncovered. After their excavation in 1971, Hassal and Hill could only conclude that it might represent a 12th century re-build of Edward's fortification or it might have been a medieval flood prevention work.

Comparison with other towns suggests that a Norman origin is more likely. Thus the King's Ditch at Hereford and the Black Ditch at Monmouth as well as the King's Ditch at Cambridge have all been ascribed to the Norman period. Writing of the last, Lobel has suggested that it was "a legal boundary and toll barrier which would separate the stricter King's peace of the town from the ordinary land peace outside". The possibility of such a Norman origin and purpose for Bedford's ditch is reinforced by the fact that St Mary's Church is first mentioned in a charter of William I dated to c1077 and this date is compatible with the oldest surviving fabric of the church. It would seem that William's purpose was to expand Bedford by building a "new town" on the south bank of the river.

Chapter 5

Religious Institutions

Newnham Priory

Another significant event took place during the reign of the first Plantagenet king, Henry II. This was to have profound and lasting effect on the town, not so much on its topography as on its economy. This was the foundation of Newnham Priory.

As discussed above, St Paul's Church was at one time a collegiate church staffed by irregular canons. The canons were termed irregular because they lived in their own homes around the town and were not bound by any monastic rule. The college of canons was in existence at least as early as the reign of Edward the Confessor and is specifically mentioned in that section of the Domesday Book that covers Bedford. St Paul's Church is, in fact, the only church in Bedfordshire to be specifically mentioned in the Domesday Book.

This system of irregular canons was to come to an abrupt end in 1164 when they were regularised in a monastic order. This followed an event which had violent repercussions on national history. At that time there were six canons at St. Paul's whose names are known to us. One of these was Nicholas, the Archdeacon, another was William who was to become the first prior of the monastery, another was Philip de Brois whose unfortunate brush with the law was to lead to the foundation of the priory. In 1164, Philip was involved in a tavern brawl in which a man was killed. Philip was arraigned for manslaughter but the court which tried him acquitted him. This was one of the events which led to the great dispute between Henry II and Thomas, Archbishop of

Canterbury. Philip had been cleared by the ancient practice of compurgation, i.e. he had found twelve honourable men willing to swear that they believed him innocent. Simon FitzPeter, sheriff of Bedfordshire, was dissatisfied with this result and attempted to re-open the case. Philip responded to this by heaping abuse on the sheriff. The sheriff had little choice but to take the matter up with the king. The king backed his sheriff and the archbishop backed his priest. The political situation on the national level culminated in the assassination of Thomas, although the law of "benefit of clergy" was to linger on for many years. On the local level it was decided that the canons of St Paul's must be put under tighter control and, in fact, be regularised under the Augustinian order. This plan was initiated by Rose, or Rohesia de Beauchamp, widow of Payne de Beauchamp. She contributed to the endowment but she died before her plan could come to fruition. Her son, Simon de Beauchamp, carried through the plan and the new priory was founded in 1166. The monastery continued to be based at St Paul's for another twelve years. It is not known how the new rule affected the living arrangements of the old canons now that they had become monks. Did they live in communal quarters for instance? If so, where? In 1178, they moved to a custom-built monastery just over the border in Goldington. The site was called "Newnham" — "the new field by the river". They had acquired the site from Alan Wintermilk who, according to Domesday, had held half a hide from King Edward the Confessor. He could grant the land "to whom he would" and he chose to give it to the canons of St. Paul's under King William and declared that they should have it altogether after his death. This half-hide, or more precisely, 60 acres, is marked on the pre-enclosure map of Goldington.

There are no physical remains of the priory buildings but archaeological investigations under way at the time of writing

Bounds of the Newnham Priory complex (abstracted from the pre-enclosure map of Goldington).

may throw some light on this. The fragments of brick wall which border the edge of the Aspects Car Park mark the boundary of the garden of the mansion which replaced the monastery after the Dissolution. A field of humps and bumps just to the south east of this marks the site of the monastic fish ponds. The sixty acres of the monastic grounds is roughly bisected by Barker's Lane. The area to the south of Barker's Lane would have contained the monastic buildings including the church. The area to the north would have contained the monastery gardens and possibly an orchard. Old walls, one length between Priory Park and Priory Marina and another alongside Barker's Lane, are believed to mark the boundaries of the priory complex. The monks had a water mill. This was situated at the eastern end of the northern reach of the river, just before it rejoins the main river.

Simon de Beauchamp granted, to the new priory, churches and lands from around the county and also fishing rights on the River Ouse. Many citizens of Bedford followed his example. This process of accumulation of property was greatly facilitated in 1310 when Edward II, at the instigation of Queen Isabella, gave the priory licence for the acquisition in mortmain of land and rents to the yearly value of £20. The latest recorded gift under this licence was when Thomas Chalton granted The Old George to the priory (see below).

Despite the violent incident which precipitated its foundation, the history of the Priory is mainly the account of this peaceful acquisition of property. Some of the early documents recording these transactions have been lost but most of them have been preserved in the Cartulary of Newnham Priory which has been transcribed and published in BHRS volume 43. Another important document, the Newham Priory Rental of 1507, has also been translated and published in BHRS vol. 25. As was the case with most monasteries, Newnham had its share of legal disputes with its neighbours and other ecclesiastical establishments. There were two occasions, for instance, when Simon de Beauchamp had to step in and defend the Priory. These involved the right to advowsons of the churches at Apsley and Hatley. There was also an occasion in 1330 when the prior was charged with raising the level of the pond at Castle Mill and so causing flooding which was a nuisance to the neighbourhood. However, it was found that the pond was justly raised so the prior was acquitted. There was also a report of a dispute between the priories of Newnham and Caldwell, though neither the issue nor the outcome is known.

One of the services the Priory provided for the town was a school. This was to prove to be arguably the most important aspect of the monastery as far as the town of Bedford was concerned. When the monastery was dissolved by Henry VIII, most of the land in the villages around Bedford was acquired by John Gostwick, but the property in the town went mostly to John Williams, alias Scott, who was Mayor of Bedford in 1546. This town property included the priory school. Williams was able to keep the school going until it was taken up by William Harpur and, eventually, it developed into the Harpur Trust Schools which have had such an influence on the later history of the town.

OTHER RELIGIOUS INSTITUTIONS

A number of other religious institutions made their appearance in or around Bedford during the late 12th to early 14th centuries. These comprised two monasteries, Caldwell Priory and the Franciscan Friary, and three hospitals, St. John's, St. Leonard's and St. Loye's. There were also two other churches, Allhallows and St. Cuthbert's whose recorded history began in this period.

Caldwell Priory

There is some confusion over the origin of Caldwell Priory. A charter of Henry II confirming an earlier charter of Henry I seems to suggest a connection between Caldwell Priory and the Countess Judith. The charters confirm all grants which had been made to the Abbey of Elstow and include one item which reads: "of the gift of Countess Judith, 12 acres of land at Caldwella and 7 acres adjoining the same place; and 12 acres in a place called Berchesdig". It is known that "Berchesdig" alias "Barkditch", alias the King's Ditch, bordered the Priory grounds but the charters imply that this is in a different place from Caldwella. Mawer and Stenton have identified a place called "Caldwella" at Hill Farm in Houghton Conquest, well to the south of Caldwell Priory. Furthermore, the Countess Judith died in 1090, well before the earliest dates suggested for the foundation of the Priory. Also, the Countess' grant was to Elstow Abbey and there is no evidence of any connection between Elstow and Caldwell. The Lysons brothers suggested that the Priory was founded during the reign of King John which lasted from 1199 to 1216, but that date can be rejected, as the Priory was definitely in existence during the reign of King Malcolm IV of Scotland (1153 to 1156), as the prior of Caldwell appears as a witness on a charter of Robert Bruce issued during that reign. Dugdale suggested the eighteenth year of King Stephen i.e. 1153. Both the Lysons and Dugdale agree that the priory was founded by one Simon Bascot or Basket. There was a Simon Barshot serving as Mayor of Bedford sometime before 1288, so one of his ancestors might have been the founder. It is more likely though that, as Leyland suggests, one of the Beauchamp family was the founder. Simon de Beauchamp of Bedford founded Newnham Priory in 1166 and Hugh de Beauchamp of Eaton founded Bushmead Priory in 1195. Simon Barscot might have been an early patron.

When originally founded, the house was of an order of The Holy Sepulchre. This order followed the same rules as the Augustinians and, in fact, on two occasions, canons of the Augustinian Priory at Dunstable were invited to be priors at Caldwell. The order of the Holy Sepulchre fell into decay shortly after the foundation though, and was revived as an Augustinian house. It could be that Simon Barscot played an important role in that renaissance so was, in one sense, a founder.

Although of the same Augustinian order, Caldwell was a much smaller priory than Newnham. It received gifts of sites in Bedford and in the surrounding villages, but its endowments were less than half those of Newnham. In 1291 the following Bedfordshire churches belonged to Caldwell: Bromham, Roxton, Sandy and Oakley, along with a chapel at Clapham. They also held churches in other counties, including Marsworth in Buckinghamshire, Arnesby in Leicestershire and Tolleshunt Major in Essex. The temporal possessions of the priory were mainly in Bedfordshire and amounted to less than £50 in 1291. In 1336, the priory held lands and tenements in Bedford, Bromham, Milton, Colesden, Roxton, Chalverston, Sandy, Sutton, Potton, Thurleigh, Holwell, Felmersham and Shelton.

Caldwell gets a mention in a few legal records. The Coroner's roll for 1272 records that William le Cupere, with the help of a plumber, was doing repairs at Caldwell Church. While trying to catch two pigeons in the belfry, he fell and died the next day. There is also a record that a judge assigned money found in the purse of a murdered man to the value of 3s 1d. "Let them be given on the king's behalf to the canons of Caldwell". This seems to be a typical example of a deodand or "gift to God" of unclaimed money arising from a crime or accident. The priory was not always on the right side of the law. As mentioned above, the Prior was one of those accused of filling in the King's Ditch.

As the canons of the priory assisted the King, at the time of the siege of Bedford Castle, by providing stones for the mangonels, they were rewarded with a share of the stone when the castle was dismantled in 1224. Many believe that it was this stone that was used to construct the wall marking the southern boundary of the priory land that can still be seen along the northern side of the Kemptson Road. Other remains of the Priory buildings disappeared many years ago. The Lysons, writing in 1806, said that there was a farmhouse on the site and traces of the conventual buildings in a field adjoining. The Rev. C.F. Farrar, writing in 1921, disagreed vehemently with the Lysons statement. He believed that the existing building, i.e. the house that had replaced the farmhouse mentioned by the Lysons, was either part of the priory buildings or on the foundations of priory buildings. He concluded that the farmhouse was originally the chapel which had been adapted into a dwelling house and that the adjoining barn was the actual priory building. He also described how the walls that were still standing would have formed part of the original cloisters. His arguments seem reasonable enough, but he admits "I am no antiquarian or archaeologist". As all the buildings have now gone, only archaeological excavation will throw any light on whether his conclusions were correct.

When the priory was dissolved in 1535/36, Thomas Dey was the prior, and with him were six canons and two lay brothers. Its yearly income was £109. 8s. 5d. After the dissolution the property was administered, on behalf of the King, by Sir John Gostwick. It was demised to William Gostwick and his wife Anne by an indenture dated December 3rd 1537, for a period of 21 years. William Gostwick was the younger brother of Sir John. The property was described as "consisting of all messages, outbuildings, barns, dovecotes, gardens hortis, orchards, gardinis, lands and ground within site and ambit and circuit of said late Priory". The property then went to Thomas Leigh of London by an indenture dated September 14th 1546. He became Mayor of Bedford in 1556. At the beginning of the 19th century it was owned by George Livius and was not broken up into lots until the 20th century.

Greyfriars Friary

The arrival of the Greyfriars or Franciscans can be dated with some precision. The Franciscan order had been founded by St Francis of Assisi in 1210. The members came to be called Greyfriars because of the colour of the habit they wore. They came to England in 1224 and were established in Bedford very soon after that. The Bedford Greyfriars received a grant of wood from the King in 1238. They had a church, dedicated in 1295, but they saw their mission as spreading the word of God to as many people as possible. For that reason they tended to do their preaching at crosses in the open air. They had a preaching cross in Forth Street (now Midland Road), which was connected to the Friary by a footpath known as Greyfriars Walk. This followed,

Greyfriars Friary – from an engraving by the Buck brothers
mistakenly captioned by them as Newnham Priory.

very roughly, the line of the modern thoroughfare known as Greyfriars.

Their policy of direct approach to the people made them very popular. Chaucer's friar is portrayed as a merry rogue, with a twinkle in his eye for the ladies, who did not allow his vows of poverty to weigh too heavily on him. They found favour with more influential people as well as the commoners. According to Leyland, a number of such people were buried within their church at Bedford. These included Lord Mowbray, Sir Richard Irencester, who is said to have built the main body of the church, and Mabel Pateshall of Bletsoe. Leland named the latter as founder of the friary, but the only lady of that name known did not live until the 14th century. Leland also mentions a tomb for Queen Eleanor, although the three queens of that name were all dead before the church had been dedicated. Margaret de Crioll expressed a wish to be buried in the church of the friars minor in Bedford in her will of 1319. She was grandmother of John de Pabenham who was married to Agnes de Pateshall, heiress to part of the Beauchamp barony of Bedford.

The friary was dissolved in 1538 and granted to John Gostwick in 1540. In a letter to Thomas Cromwell, acknowledging this grant, Gostwick made the cynical comment, "The King will have great benefit there in lead and other things" Gostwick did not retain the property long but, almost immediately, alienated it to William Borne. Since then it passed through various hands till by the time of the Enclosure of 1795 it was in the possession of Lord Ashburnham. It then comprised some 35 acres of land with a homestead and garden. The Lysons, writing at the end of the 18th century, stated that "the few remains which still exist of the conventual buildings exhibit some vestiges of the cloisters. A barn adjoining to the house is said to have been the refectory". A picture by the Buck Brothers described as "Newnham Priory" is probably of the friary, as it carries the inscription "now the property of Lord Ashburnham" who was by then the owner of the property. The outline of the friary buildings shown on Reynolds map of 1841 corresponds nicely with that illustration.

St. John's Hospital

This was the earliest of the religious hospitals of Bedford to be founded but it is the only one of which any fabric remains. By a strange coincidence, the surviving building is, at the time of writing, serving as the headquarters of the Bedford unit of the St John's Ambulance Brigade, but there is no historical connection. Nor is there any connection between the Bedford hospital and the Knights Hospitaller of St John which had been founded in Jerusalem some 60 years before.

It was not a hospital in the medical sense, more of an almshouse. Again there is some uncertainty about the precise date of its foundation. Dates ranging from 980 to 1280 have been suggested but it is now generally accepted that it was founded by Robert de Parys in about 1180. This fits in well with the first mention of the hospital in 1216. Robert de Parys laid down rules on how he wanted the hospital to be run. There would be only three brethren to staff the place. These included one acting as Master. They were to sing, every day, the canonical hours and celebrate the Divine offices for the living and the dead. They were to eat in the hall and sleep in the dormitory. They were to have their hair cut to the tonsure of a priest and wear decent clothing covered by a black mantle. On their admission they were to swear obedience to the Master and were to stay in the hospital all their lives. They were to pray for the soul of the founder, Robert de Parys, and for the souls of the benefactors, John and Henry Saint John and John le Neve, also anyone else who had given rents or possessions or who would give them in the future.

Robert de Parys declared that all poor men of Bedford who were of free birth and had come to poverty through no fault of their own, would be charitably received but men from outside Bedford would not be received. It would be unlawful for the Mayor, Bailiffs or Burgess of the Borough to admit poor men to the hospital unless Robert de Parys or his successors had interviewed them and given their consent. Robert took the precaution of having a copy of his ordinance kept in the common chest of the town in case the original was destroyed by fire.

In the Valor Ecclesiasticus of 1535, the hospital was assessed at £21.0s.8d. It appears to have escaped the Dissolution. This may be because it had ceased to function as a hospital by then. An enquiry at the end of Henry VIII's reign into the condition of chantries and hospitals revealed that no poor person was kept there nor had been for many years. The value at that time was assessed at £20. The old foundation must have continued to provide support for poor people in the community although not resident in the hospital. At the end of the 18th century, ten beadsmen were receiving 9d per week from the hospital funds. The rectors of St. John's Church continued to be Masters of the Hospital until 1881 when the Hospital Estate was wound up by Act of Parliament.

The Hospital building, now called St John's House, is of medieval origin but has undergone many changes over the years. Parts of its fabric date back to its foundation in the late 12th century. A lot of the timber construction appears to be late 15th or 16th centuries.

St Leonard's Hospital

Unlike St John's this was a medical hospital. It was situated just outside the southern boundary of the town. Again, the precise date of its foundation is not known but the earliest mention is in the charter of King John dated 1207. This granted the brethren and preachers safe conduct to go around England collecting alms for the hospital. The charter refers to "fraters hospitales infirmorum", i.e. "brethren of the hospital for sick people". A later charter, of 1215, refers more specifically to "leprosos hospitalis Sci Leonardi", i.e. it was a leper hospital. This is why it was situated outside the town.

It has been suggested that the founder was a man called Basset, probably of the same family who was involved in the early history of Caldwell Priory. Initially it was staffed by six brethren, one of whom served as Master. They wore the habits of religion and probably observed a similar rule to that prevailing at St. John's Hospital. They underwent some degree of expansion in the early 14th century. In 1302, the Brethren petitioned Parliament for permission to purchase land to the value of £10 together with a rent in Bedford. This was followed in 1306 by a request for permission to close a lane that was running through the middle of their site because they now had buildings on both sides of it. The Master considered it to be a security risk, exposing their buildings to the greater possibility of theft. (Also, one imagines it would have been thought a health risk to people using the lane). The Abbess of Elstow opposed the closure because the lane was well used by her people travelling to and fro between Bedford and the Abbey. The court decided that the closure could go ahead if an alternative route was provided which was not substantially longer than the original. A route was provided and this, after careful measurement, proved to be slightly longer, by some 10 poles (165 ft). This was thought to be acceptable by the court, and permission for closure was granted. The abbess continued to press her case though, first with Edward I then with his son Edward II, but the judgement against her was upheld and the lane was closed.

This success seems to have marked the high point in the hospital's existence and shortly afterwards it seems to have gone into a decline. By 1331, the hospital was granted an indulgence for the repair of the chapel and in 1353 it was given a licence to beg for alms. Nevertheless, it continued until well into the 16th century. The Newnham Priory Rental of 1507 mentions the Master of St Leonard's eight times, indicating that the hospital held several properties around the town and fields of Bedford. Those mentioned in the Rental include part of the Swan Inn, tenements and tofts in St. Peter's parish and land in Middle Field and Bury Field. The Valor Ecclesiasticum of 1535, which gives an assessment just before the Dissolution, valued the hospital at £20-6-4¾d. It seems to have survived the Dissolution and it is not listed in the Accounts of Augmentations which followed. During the brief Catholic interlude under Mary I, the Archbishop, Cardinal Pole, made a visitation and reported that the hospital had been "violated and occupied by Laymen a great while in the time of the schism". England returned to the Protestant fold with the accession of Elizabeth I and, in 1575, she granted the site of the hospital to one Richard Senhouse. After that St. Leonard's passed through the hands of various lay persons until it was finally acquired by the Duke of Bedford in 1750. During this period it became known as St. Leonard's Farm. A map of 1773 shows the position of the farm and gives a clue to the site of the earlier hospital. It was in the area bounded by Elstow Road, Ampthill Road and London Road, near the Old St John's Railway Station. The name is remembered today by the street names, St Leonard's Avenue and St Leonard's Street. Although completely surrounded by St Mary's parish, it was part of the enclave of St John's parish which comprised St John's Church itself, the hospital pertaining to St John's, St Leonard's Hospital and a corridor of land connecting these. With the coming of the

St Leonard's Farm before it was demolished in 1846.

railway to Bedford in 1846, the farm was finally demolished to make way for the Bedford to Bletchley line. There is an interesting report in the Bedfordshire Times describing a supper laid on by Mr Austin of St Leonard's Farm for the workmen employed on the Bedford Terminus — "It was a strange contrast to see sixty three hearty fellows assembled in jovial concourse and reflect that some centuries back the same room was used by the Monks of St Leonard". Unless the author of the report was allowing his romantic imagination to run away with him, this implies that at least part of the fabric of the hospital had survived as part of the farm buildings. A drawing reproduced in Farrar's "Old Bedford" certainly lends support to this idea. The gate shown in the drawing might well be across the old lane that was the subject of the 14th century closure dispute.

St Loye's

This was the other religious institution which provided a medical function. The chapel of St Loye's stood on the site later occupied by Trinity Church. This itself became part of the Bedford High School for Girls. The pest house stood adjacent to it.

Loye, or Elois as he was known in France, was born in the late 6th century. As a boy he was apprenticed to a goldsmith and showed such skill and artistry that he was soon noticed by the king, Clothair II. Clothair showed him a storeroom packed with gold and precious stones and commissioned him to use as much as he needed to make a bejewelled throne. Elois made two thrones and returned the key of the store to the king with most of the contents untouched. The king was so impressed by this scrupulous honesty, as rare then as it is now, that he took him into his service. He rose to become Master of the Mint. Elois used this position to benefit the Church and eventually he was made Bishop of Noyon. It is during his time in this office, while he was on missionary work in the pagan lands to the north of France, that he performed the miracle for which he is best remembered. He was challenged to replace a shoe on a mad horse which no one else had dared to approach. Elois tackled the problem by detaching the leg of the horse, replacing the shoe and then putting the leg back in place on the horse. A bas-relief in Durweston Church in Dorset shows St Loye in the act of performing this miracle on a rather docile-looking little horse. On the strength of this miracle he was adopted as patron saint of farriers and other trades associated with horses. In his Friar's Tale, Chaucer makes the carter invoke St Loye when his horse, after a long struggle, is able to pull the cart out of a muddy patch. As a result of his success as a goldsmith St Loye was made patron saint of metal workers. His cult was introduced into England when Edward III took Philippa of Hainault as his wife in 1328. Philippa's sister

St Loye performing his miracle in a bas-relief in Durweston Church, Dorset.

was prioress at a convent near Stratford-at-Bow. Once again we can find an interesting allusion in Chaucer's Canterbury Tales. He tells us in the prologue that the prioress spoke the French of Stratford atte Bow, "Frensh of Parys was to hire unknown". This is generally interpreted as a slur on the prioress' education, but in another line Chaucer hints at another explanation. He tells us that the prioress' only oath was by St Loy. Could Chaucer be making a political comment here? The Count of Hainault was at that time working towards independence from France, so his daughters would hardly be favourable towards Paris.

Following the introduction of his cult into England, trade guilds for smiths and farriers were dedicated to him in all parts of England. Healing powers for humans as well as for horses were attributed to him and chapels dedicated to St Loye were attached to hospitals, especially those dealing with infectious diseases. These were known as pest houses and were usually built on the edge of the towns away from the general populace. Such was the case in Bedford. There is a carving of St Loye, holding his hammer in one hand and a horse's leg in the other, high in the rafters of St Paul's Church.

Allhallows Church

This church, also known as All Saints Church, is clearly marked on Speed's map standing adjacent to, and on the west side of, Allhallows Lane at its northern end. Unlike St Peter's to the north and St Cuthbert's to the east, this church does not show any obvious relation to the Saxon burh. The western entrance to the burh would have been at the end of Well Street at the southern end of Allhallows Lane. Allhallows Church is at the northern end of that road. So it is not known when Allhallows had been founded. It was certainly in existence in the 12th century when the Abbey of Missenden quitclaimed its rights in the church to

St Paul's. At that time it had its own graveyard. This is referred to in an item in the cartulary of Harrold Priory dated 1260/70, which mentions "the way which leads from the cemetery of All Saints toward Colleswell". Archaeological evidence for the graveyard was revealed when graves were uncovered during the pedestrianisation of Allhallows Street in 1988. The church continued to be administered as a separate parish with its own rectory and advowson until it was merged with St Paul's in the 17th century. The church itself must have been demolished sometime towards the end of the 17th century when Christie Almshouses were built on the site. The geographical area of the parish cannot be precisely defined. Land listed in the Newnham Priory Rental of 1507 indicates that parts, at least, of Conduit Field which lay on the western side of the town, must have been in Allhallows parish. This suggests that the parish extended to the west, possibly as far as the boundary with Clapham. On the other hand, these particular parcels of land may have been extra-parochial as so many were in the Middle Ages. One croft, for instance, was listed in Cucking Stool Lane, which was known to be on the other side of the town at the southern end of Kimbolton Road.

St Cuthbert's Church

This church stood, approximately at least, on the site of the present church at the eastern end of Mill Street. This was near the eastern entry to the Saxon burh so suggests an early origin for the church. It has been argued that the dedication to St Cuthbert is further evidence for this early origin, but it would be unusual for an early church to be dedicated to anyone other than one of the New Testament saints unless the saint had strong local connections.

As far as we know, the cult of St Cuthbert never penetrated so far south as Bedford, so we have to look to a later period for an explanation of the dedication. The known history of the church begins with references to it in the cartulary of Dunstable Priory in the middle of the 12th century. Dr G.H. Fowler, who edited the transcript of the cartulary for the Bedford Historical Record Society, concluded that the church had been founded at about the date of those references. It may be more than coincidence that a prior of Dunstable in office around that time was a man named Cuthbert. Of course, this does not rule out the possibility that there had been an earlier church on the same site.

The present church is a 19th century rebuild, but there are illustrations and descriptions of an earlier building which was demolished in 1845. Sir Stephen Glynne, writing sometime before 1840, described the church thus, "this is a small mean fabric comprising only a nave and a chancel. There is no steeple but a wooden turret rises above the roof about the middle of the church. There is one lancet window on the south side, the others are chiefly of late Curvilinear character. The north doorway is Early English, with good mouldings and shafts. The chancel is separated from the nave by three arches of wood. On the south side of the altar are two Early English niches with extremely good mouldings and divided by a central shaft. The font is circular, supported by four shafts standing on a square base. The interior is neatly paved".

This description is compatible with a number of illustrations of this earlier church. The font, though, is the only feature which has survived and this can still be seen in the rebuilt church, although the one in use today is a more modern one. The old font has been dated by various authorities as Saxon, Norman or 14th century.

According to Ralf de Coggeshall, St Cuthbert's, like St Paul's, suffered from the depredations of Falkes de Breaute during his occupation of the castle. So parts, at least, would have been

St. Cuthbert's church as it was before the nineteenth century rebuild.

rebuilt some time after the demolition of the castle in 1224.

A probable architectural history of the church could be sketched out as follows. Assuming there was a church contemporary with the Saxon burh this would almost certainly have been of wood. There must have been a Norman church to correspond with the dates given in the Dunstable cartulary, i.e. mid 12th century, and this would have been the one ravished by Faulkes de Breaute in the early 13th century. The Early English features described by Sir Stephen Glynne would date from the reconstruction of the church after the demolition of the castle, and his "curvilinear" features, presumably in the style of the Decorated Period, would have been later alterations. The present church represents the complete rebuild of the mid 19th century.

PART THREE

Late
Medieval
Bedford

17th century onwards

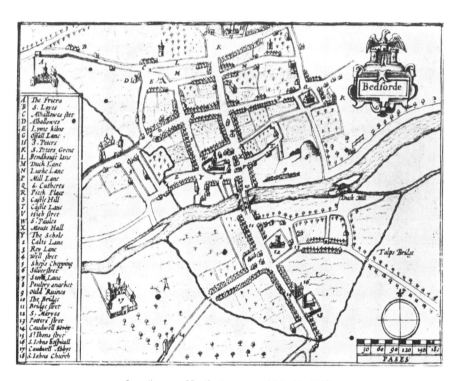

The following is the key/legend visible on the left side of the map:

A	The Friers
B	S. Loyes
C	Alhallowes stret
D	Alhallowes
E	Lyme kilne
G	Offall Lane
H	S. Peters
K	S. Peters Grene
L	Bendhouse lane
M	Duck Lane
N	Lurke Lane
P	Mill Lane
Q	S. Cutherts
R	Picch Place
S	Castle Hill
T	Castle Lane
V	High stret
W	S. Paules
X	Moote Hall
Y	The Schole
1	Calts Lane
2	Rey Lane
3	Well stret
4	Shep's Chepping
5	Silver stret
6	Sow Lane
7	Poultry amarket
8	oild Ruines
9	The Bridge
10	Bridge stret
11	S. Maryes
12	Potters stret
13	Cauduell stret
14	S. Ihens stret
15	S. Iohns hospitall
16	Cauduell Abbye
17	S. Iohns Church

Bedforde

Duck Mill

Talps Bridge

PASES
30 60 90 120 140 180

Speed's map of Bedford town – published in 1610.

Chapter 6

John Speed's Bedford

About seventy years after the last of the events described in Part Two, John Speed was publishing his maps of the counties of Britain. These were mostly copied, with only minor alterations, from the work of earlier cartographers like Christopher Saxon. But Speed included, as insets in the corners of his county maps, plans of the principal towns of each county. These were his own work, based on his own surveys. Bedford town plan, published in 1610, is one of these.

The map has been reproduced many times and makes an attractive feature to hang on the wall, but it is rather more than that.

The accuracy of Speed's surveying was not to be equalled until Reynolds published his map of the town in 1841. This accuracy can be tested in two ways; firstly, by the relative bearings of landmarks taken from a suitable survey point; and secondly, by the distances of these landmarks from a chosen point.

To check the first, we can go through an armchair-surveying exercise. Imagine that we have set up a plane table on the castle mound and have laid out sightlines to the six churches which would have been visible to Speed from that point. We can do this with the help of the modern Ordnance Survey map. With a piece of tracing paper, we can draw out various sightlines. When we superimpose the tracing paper onto Speed's map, we find that the sightlines run neatly through each of the churches. Where Speed does fall down is on orientation. Speed's compass indicator, in the bottom right of the map, is about 10 degrees east of the true north as shown on the O.S. map. This means that the sight lines tracing has to be rotated through that amount in order to make it fit. When we apply the same exercise to later town maps, e.g. Jefferys' of 1765 or Cole's of 1807, it proves impossible to fit the land marks onto the sightlines no matter how we adjust the orientation. Speed also comes out comparatively well on the distance test. The table shows the distances in yards from St Peter's Church to the other churches as shown on the respective maps. The distances have been measured from the maps and then translated into yards according to the scales shown on each map. Speed's "pase" has been taken to be equivalent to 5¼ ft.

Distances, in yards, from St. Peter's to various other churches in Bedford as shown on various town maps

	St. Paul's	St. Cuthbert's	St. Mary's	St. John's
O.S.	495	342	786	991
Speed	488	378	781	1015
Jefferys	483	402	816	1041
Cole	643	500	1014	1236
Reynolds	487	385	791	1007

When it comes to detail, Speed tends to resort to conventional symbolism. The streets are shown as impossibly wide, as they are on a modern A–Z street map. The built-up streets are shown as bird's eye views of long terraces of little identical houses. The larger buildings such as The Friary, Caldwell Priory and Hassets are all shown as typical Tudor mansions. The monasteries had long ceased to be used as such, but records show that both the Friary and Caldwell had shown their monastic form to a large extent till after Speed's day. The Tudor mansion is appropriate for Hassets as that is what it was. (Hassets is not named on Speed's map, but from other references it can be identified with the mansion shown towards the western end of Well Street). Speed has shown the churches individually with a spire for St. Paul's, the towers for St John's and St Mary's. St Cuthbert's is shown with a little bell turret, just as it appears in early drawings. He also shows several minor details in the right places e.g. a well in Wells Street, a lime kiln in Lime Street and a pillory and market cross in the High Street.

But the most useful aspect of Speed's map is that it shows the rectilinear street plan which had been laid down in Saxon times and which can still be picked out in the streets which form the central core of modern Bedford. Speed's map is the last map to be published before Bedford started to expand in the 18th and 19th centuries. It therefore represents the final stage of what can be called Medieval Bedford.

The Bounds of the Medieval Town

Nothing remains of the physical boundaries of the Saxon burh, but the pattern of the rectilinear pattern of its streets strongly indicates that its borders correspond to what, at one stage, formed the boundaries of St Paul's parish. Thus the eastern boundary of the burh ran along the parish boundary between St Paul's and St Cuthbert's; the northern boundary corresponds to that between St Paul's and St Peter's. The western boundary is more problematical, as the one-time boundary between St Paul's and Allhallows was lost when those two parishes were merged. However, it can be deduced from descriptions of some of the properties in that part of the town. These indicate that the boundary probably ran along Allhallows Street. Thus properties to the east of that line are allotted to St Paul's while those to the west lay in Allhallows. The southern boundary of the original burh was formed, of course, by the River Ouse.

It is important to remember how small the Saxon and medieval town was compared to the modern town. It stretched from Allhallows in the west to St Cuthbert's in the east, about 540 metres, and from St Peter's in the north to St John's in the south, about 1000 metres. This compares to modern Bedford which spans about 4000 metres east to west and some 5000 metres north to south. Most of the area occupied by the modern town was covered with the common fields worked by the townsfolk and which supplied them with food and other basic necessities. We will look at these fields later. Firstly, we will look in detail at the streets of the medieval town, some of the principal buildings and some of the people who lived there.

The High Street

The axis of the old town was, as it is today, the High Street. This is the only street which still forms a continuous north to south route, crossing the river near to the original ford. As described above, it can be traced from Clapham Park, past the old cemetery, down Foster Hill Road, down the centre of the town and over the bridge. It then continued on to the south. Records show that it has always served as the High Street to the town or "alta strata" in Latin documents.

St Peter's Church

Just before it entered the old town, the street passed near to St Peter's Church, appropriately dedicated to the Saint who held the keys to Heaven. In fact it has been suggested that Saint Peter's once formed part of the defences of the burh, guarding the gate as St Martin's Church does at Wareham, for instance. This is unlikely, though, as it lies well to the east of the Foster Hill/High Street line. It is more likely that it was an extra-mural church which had collected its own market place on St Peter's Green.

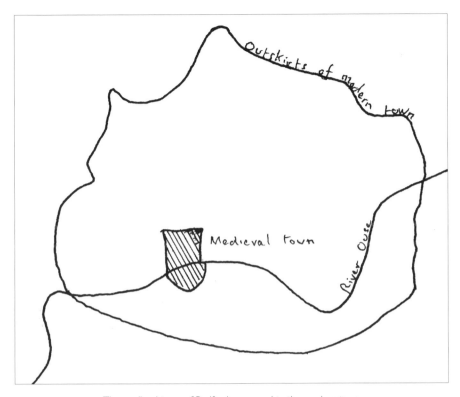

The medieval town of Bedford compared to the modern town.

This is supported by the fact that in the 14th century it was known as St Peter-in-Campis, i.e. St Peter-in-the-Fields. The Green has been known under that name for at least 400 years. Wool fairs were held there in the medieval period and these were revived in 1852 and continued to be held for twenty years. At one time, though, the graveyard must have extended over the Green, as evidence of burials was uncovered when the Bunyan statue was being erected. Burials were also found when a subterranean chamber was constructed for an electrical installation and again when air-raid shelters were built during World War II.

As a building, the church is one of the oldest in the town. The tower and chancel are both of Saxon origin, showing traces of long and short work in the quoins probably dating to the 10th or 11th centuries. Taylor and Taylor have suggested that it is a late Saxon tower erected on top of an earlier structure.

The church was granted to Merton Priory in Surrey some time during the 12th century. Exactly when or by whom is not known but it was certainly in the possession of Merton in 1170. Merton Priory had been founded in 1121, so it acquired St Peter's quite early in its existence.

Bendhouse Lane

Running west from opposite St Peter's Green is the street now known as Dame Alice Street. In earlier times it was called Bendhouse Lane. That is the name used on Speed's map, for instance. This is now a well-used thoroughfare leading out of Bedford to the west along the Bromham Road. But this was not always the case. As discussed above, the indications are that both Bromham Road and Dame Alice Road/Bendhouse Lane were developed later than the field system on that side of the town. The name "Bendhouse Lane" is a reference to what was one of Bedford's main industries in the medieval period, i.e. tanning. The Roll of Taxation of the Ninth of 1297 mentions eleven tanneries in Bedford. Part, at least, of this trade was practiced in the St Peter's area. There are 15th century references to a John Tanner who held property in St. Peter's parish and John West's tenement, known as Tanners, is described in a lease of 1447 as being situated in St Peter's parish alongside a ditch called Le Saffrondyche. Running water was one of the essentials for the early stages of tanning. The other was lime and this was to be had from the lime kiln shown on Speed's map at the end of Lime Street, as it is still called. In the final stages of the tanning process, "the hides are stretched over one another with weights atop to keep them tight and straight; and in this condition are sold under the denomination of bend leather". A bend is defined as the thickest and stoutest kind of leather used for the soles of boots and shoes. The bend-house, therefore, would have been the site of the final stage of leather production or as a warehouse where the finished bends were stored. A deed of 1559 refers to "a tenement lately termed a barn" situated in Marstons Lane. This was another name for Bendhouse Lane, so the barn referred to could well have been the bendhouse.

Lime Street and Lurke Street

The lime kiln used by the tanners was approached along Lime Street. This ran roughly parallel to Bendhouse Lane and a little to its south. Opposite to it, across the High Street, is Lurke Street, running east. It has been suggested that these two streets together formed an "intramural lane" running just inside the northern defences of the Saxon burh. As there is no precise evidence of the position of those defences, this can only be speculative, but it is supported by the fact that the boundary between the parishes of St Peter's and St Paul's Churches lies along the northern side of the two streets. Also the streets together form the most northerly of the east-west streets of the burh grid pattern. Lime Street led to the lime kiln but "Lurke Street" is more of a mystery. It has retained its name from, at least, the 15th century with only minor variations of spelling. In the 15th century it was spelled "Lurclane". But the significance of the name remains open to speculation.

Robert Cuckoo's House

Not far to the south of Lurke Lane, Speed's map shows a large building facing onto the High Street. This is not just cartographer's licence on Speed's part. The same building appears again on

Jeffery's map of 1765 and on Brayley's map of 1807. It appears again on Reynold's map of 1841 but, by that time, it had been broken down into smaller tenements. It is unfortunate that no illustrations of the building have survived, apart from Speed's little sketch which shows it to have been a plain rectangular building. It must have been a substantial building, some 124ft long. In the early 16th century it was occupied by Robert Cuckoo who was Mayor of Bedford in 1506. He also owned most of the land to the east of the house, lying between Lurke Street and Mill Street and extending from the High Street to the boundary of St Cuthbert's parish. All the property, including the house, was still in the hands of a single family, the Southouses, at the time of the enclosure award of 1796.

Mill Street and School Lane

Mill Street ran, as it does today, from the High Street to St Cuthbert's Church and so led to the eastern entrance to the Saxon burh. The street took its name from a horse mill which stood approximately on the site of the Bunyan Meeting Church. The street had been known as Horsemylne Lane in the 13th century. In his paper on "Bedford Town and Townsmen in 1507", W. Glassby referred to a court case of 1608 concerning "a moult mill in Bedford called Trinity Mill, worked by a horse". The brotherhood of the Trinity of Bedford was founded to maintain a chaplain to sing divine service in St Paul's Church. It was financed by properties belonging to the Mayor and Burgesses of Bedford Town who also appointed, and could dismiss, the chaplain. These properties included the mill. It came into possession of the King following the Dissolution. It seems that, before the Dissolution, the mill had a monopoly of grinding malt in the town. The monopoly had become gradually eroded as people took their grain to other mills or used their own querns.

It was not finally abolished until 1639 when a bill brought by the then occupier, one Leonard Bower, to enforce the monopoly, was dismissed. Before the Dissolution, Mill Street was also known as School Street after the monastic school run by Newnham Priory. The school was sited about halfway along the street on its northern side. This was the school which was eventually to be taken up by William Harpur and formed the seed from which the Harpur Trust schools grew.

Silver Street

The line of Mill Street was continued to the west, after crossing The High Street, along Silver Street. This was the beginning of the thoroughfare which ran west along Well Street (now Midland Road) and Forth Street (now Ford End Road) to a river crossing at Ford End in Biddenham. The name "Silver Street" has given rise to much speculation. "Silver Streets" occur as principal streets in many Saxon towns. They are often assumed to indicate the streets of silversmiths or the location of mints. The first known use of the name in Bedford is on Speed's map of 1610, but in view of the occurrence of the name in so many early towns it is reasonable to assume that it had a long history in Bedford. There was indeed a mint in Saxon Bedford. Aethelstan, in 928, decreed that every Saxon burh should have one. The first coin known to be minted in Bedford was of the reign of Eadwig (955 to 959) when there were five moneyers working in the town. However, it must not be assumed that the name Silver Street necessarily implies silver working or minting. In Reading, for instance, the name derives from "Sivekare Street" which means the street of the sievemakers. Also, the name occurs in many villages where one would not expect any working of precious metal to take place. These include, for instance, Great Barford and Stevington in Bedfordshire.

The Old George

A little to the south of Silver Street, also on the western side of the High Street, stood another very important building of medieval Bedford. This came to be known as "The Old George" and is probably the oldest lay building in the town of which any fabric remains. What does remain is now used as a storeroom by Debenhams and can be seen from the passage which runs between Silver Street and St Paul's Square.

The earliest known detailed description of "the messuage called the George" is in a deed of sale dated 1788. Essentially, it consisted of a complex of buildings grouped round a yard, referred to in the deed as an upper yard. This opened, at its eastern end, onto the High Street through what appears in early 20th century photographs as a brick arch. The northern side of the yard was occupied by ancillary buildings including a brewhouse, cooperage, granary and stables. The accommodation part of the inn occupied the southern side of the yard. This side was the site, in more recent years, of a public house known as the Old George. This was closed in 1928 and demolished in 1937 to allow for the expansion of E.P. Rose's department store, now Debenham's. A photograph of the public house taken in 1914 shows it to have been a modest building with no indication of antiquity, but the son of the last licensee, Mr Cyril Whitbread, remembered stone vaulted cellars running under the building that suggests it was on the site of an earlier and more substantial building.

At the western end of the upper yard was a stone building with a central archway leading into the lower yard which backed onto property in Harpur Street, known as Angel Street at the time of the 18thcentury deed. The arched building is described in the deed as "the old building which was formerly a chapel". At the time of the deed it comprised "a stable under the old chapel with rooms, granaries, chambers and lofts over it". It is the lower part of this building which has survived. Over the years this has acquired the name "The Old George", but it must be remembered that this is only a fragment of "The Messuage of the George Inn" and not the inn itself.

The old building has been the subject of several 18th and 19th century pictures and later photographs. The earliest known example is a pen and ink drawing by John Carter, dated 1783. This shows the building to be in a dilapidated state. The drawing has the caption, "East view of an ancient Edifice in the George Inn Yard at Bedford" (appears to have been an entrance or Gateway but said to have been a chapel dedicated to St. George)".

Cary Elwes gives a description of the interior of the building as it was in 1881. He describes the upper storey as being divided into two rooms, each having a separate entrance via external stone staircases on either side of the arch on the western side of the building, with one large hall over the arch between two small passages. This description was confirmed by a survey carried out by the architect, Mr George P Allen, during the years 1927 to 1929.

The survey was in connection with a proposal to reconstruct the building. Alas this scheme was never followed through and now all that is left of the building are the outside walls up to first floor height, including one side of the archway. The upper storey, including the top of the arch, has been replaced by a modern brick structure.

Cary Elwes' description and pictures by several artists indicate that the eastern façade of the building was decorated with a statue of St George and two shields, one of which carried a simple cross of St George. The device on the other shield is not clear but it seems, in John Carter's drawing at least, to have been a rampant lion. The west side of the building had no decoration but only

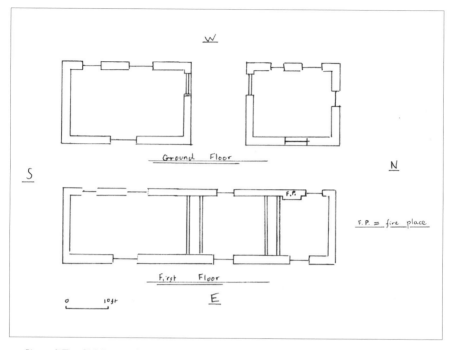

Plans of "The Old George Gatehouse" (reconstructed from various sources). The south wall of the archway was removed when the arch was widened to take traffic. Otherwise all the features of the ground floor were still in existence when the site was viewed by the author in the mid 1990s. The first floor has, of course, been completely replaced by a modern brick structure.

featured the two outside staircases leading up to the upper storey. All this implies that the archway was intended to be entered from the eastern side and that the western side was the inner side. Thus the archway was not intended as an entrance to the "messuage of the George Inn", which was entered through the other arch from the High Street.

This raises the questions: What was the original function of the arch and did it exist before the inn? Even in the surviving fragment there is some evidence that the answer to the second question might be "Yes". The top of the surviving stone work on

The Old George Gatehouse as it appears in the early 19th century.

top The rear view of The Old George Gatehouse as it appears today.

above The top right-hand corner of the surviving stonework, showing the long-and-short quoining.

Window on the north wall of The Old George Gatehouse

– a 15th-century window replacing an earlier window with a semi-circular arch.

the southern corner includes a quoin arrangement reminiscent of Saxon long-and-short work, while the window on the north wall, although 15th century in style, has obviously been inserted into an older window with a semi-circular arch of an earlier age. Cary Elwes expressed a similar opinion that the transitional style windows were probably "insertions into an older building, as the walls and roof appear of an earlier period".

With regard to the first question, i.e. what was the original purpose of the building? Farrar, writing in his book "Old Bedford", suggested that the building was the "prioratus", i.e.

the town office of the Prior of Newnham. However, this can be dismissed as a misreading of the deed where the term occurs, as that document makes it clear that the "prioratus" was "in the field of Bedford" not in the town centre and was almost certainly a reference to the buildings of the Priory itself at Newnham. But at least Farrar was aware that the building had an existence, and importance, before it became part of an inn. In fact the design of the building leaves no doubt that it was a gatehouse. This is compatible with, for instance, Carter's description in the caption to his picture and it would explain the early references to a chapel, as it was not unusual for chapels to be incorporated into gatehouses. (Compare, for example, the gatehouse at Someries near Luton). As the gatehouse was designed to be entered from the east, it must have marked the entrance to an estate of some importance on its western side. No trace of any other building related to this estate remains. Something is known though about some of the occupants of "the messuage called the George". Towards the end of the 15th century, it was held by Thomas Chalton, aka Cholton, and later by Richard Illyngworth. Chalton was a leading member of the Mercers Company of London. He was Sheriff of London in 1433 and Lord Mayor in 1449. He died in 1452. Sir Richard Illyngworth was Chief Baron of the Exchequer in 1462. He was an Honorary Member of the Mercers Company by virtue of that office. He married Thomas Chalton's widow. The George is mentioned in his Ipm of 1476. (An Ipm or Inquisition post mortem was ordered by the monarch whenever one of his tenants-in-chief died. A tenant-in-chief was one who held land directly from the monarch). The George was passed to Newnham Priory "by licence of the king" and it is listed as Priory property in the Rental of 1507. The reference to "licence of the king" presumably means the licence granted to Newnham Priory by Edward II in 1310 for acquisition, in mortmain, of land and rents to the yearly value of £20. An entry in the Patent Rolls for 1482 refers to a licence for Newnham to acquire, in mortmain, two messuages in the highway in the parish of St. Paul's Bedford some time of Thomas Chalton in part satisfaction of a licence to acquire £20 worth of land —— by letters patent of Edward II". The George remained with the Priory until the Dissolution when it became the property of John Williams alias Scott, the man who had acquired several items of Newnham property around Bedford Town, including the Priory School. Subsequently, it was to pass through various private hands.

The Market Cross and the Pillory

A little further south down the High Street, Speed's map shows two structures standing in the middle of the highway. These represent the Market Cross and the Pillory. There are references to both these in documents dating to the middle of the 13th century but the exact position of them at that time is not known. They had both been moved to the positions shown on Speed's map in 1417. The pillory was set up "nearer to the Gayhole", (i.e. the gaol). The cross had been set up "further north". Before the move, it had been located near to "a way towards P'uctone or Thuuicton". Neither of these places has been located but it can be assumed that they are one and the same, the "P" of P'uctone being a transcription error for the letter in the Old English alphabet representing the modern Th.

The later position of the pillory can be fixed with some precision because of its being adjacent to the pillory pump. This is mentioned in documents from 1700 as standing alongside the pillory itself. The pump survived longer than the pillory and can be picked out in 19th century pictures. A drawing by Fisher, for instance, dated 1820, shows the pump, as does a photograph of the High Street taken in the late 1860s. These both show the pump standing on the edge of the footpath on the western side of the street, more or less level with what is now the southern limit of Debenham's premises. This corresponds well with the position of the pillory shown on Speed's map.

St Paul's Square

At its southern end, just before it reaches the bridge, the High Street opens out into St. Paul's Square. During the Middle Ages and right through to the early 19th century, the square was filled with a maze of little streets in which various produce dealers plied their trade. On the eastern side, between the churchyard and the High Street, and running parallel to the latter, was Fish Row. The northern side was occupied by the Pig Market. This stood at the north-western end of Butcher Row which ran on an east to west line just north of the churchyard. Gooseditch Lane ran parallel to Butcher Row and just to the north of it.

Some idea of the "organised chaos" of a medieval market can be deduced from the 16th century "Black Book of Bedford", which includes regulations for "the cleane kepynge of the Bocherow":

In Primis, that every bocher of the said Towne shall erly in the mornynges and late in the evenings convey and carry awaye all the Inwards and Intrayles of beasts slautered in the Shambles or bocherowe ther and kepe cleane the nether end of the same Shambles or bocherowe where as they make their dryfte of Cattel which is at the West ende of the Tenements called the Church House so that they doe not annoye the Inhabyters thereunto adjoining withe any Corropte Savoyr or smell by Reason if the said Intrayles upon peyn to forfeit for every default to the Chamber iiijs and to the Mayor other iijs and iiijd and that they cleanse and kepe cleane their bloodd boles and Carry their Intrayle and garbeges dalye the same day the beast be killed into Offal Lane so that they kepe clene their bocherow upon the lyke payn for every offender.

Offal Lane was just outside the town to the north west and was part of what is now Tavistock Street. During the early 19th century, when that part of the town was being developed as the fashionable end of the town, the name was gentrified into "Offa Street".

The Poultry Market, according to Speed's map, occupied the south side of the square. At the eastern end of this was a group of buildings known as The Cury. In Cambridge the area known as Petit Curie was devoted to the sale of pies and other cooked goods. However the tenants listed in the Newnham Priory Rental of 1507 as occupying The Cury in Bedford do not bring such activities to mind. These include, for instance, Sir John St John and the Prior of Caldwell.

The house plots lining the southern side of the Square and running down to the river are shown on the Enclosure map of 1795 to have the long narrow shape of the burgage plots of a Saxon town. This suggests a continuity of property boundaries lasting from the earliest days of the town until comparatively recent times. Two plots, in particular, show a more specific sort of continuity. One is the Priest's Chamber. This was the home of the chaplain appointed by the prior of Newnham to administer St Paul's Church. The position of this house can be deduced from the priory Rental of 1507. In 1528, about a decade before the priory was dissolved, an indenture was drawn up between the prior and the Bishop of Lincoln appointing a vicar, to be chosen by the bishop to replace the chaplain appointed by the prior. Under the agreement, "the Vicar shall have by name his Vicarage, for his Mansion, a house of the said religious (i.e. Newnham Priory) in the said parish of St Paul's called the Priest's House. The last chaplain was a man called Sir Alexander, appointed in 1508", and the first vicar was John Berde, appointed in 1528. The Enclosure Award of 1795 lists the Rev. Thomas Gadsby

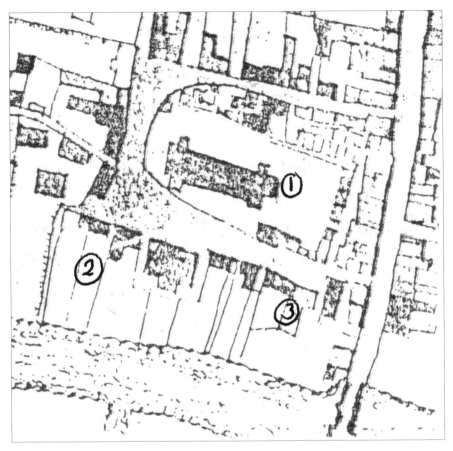

Detail from the enclosure award map showing residual burgage plots
along the south side of St. Paul's Square.

1. St. Paul's Church 2. The Vicarage, formerly the Priest's House

3. "The Ship" – formerly the Seven Stars, formerly the Falcon

as proprietor of the vicarage which it shows to be on the site
previously occupied by the Priest's House. The vicarage remained
on that site until 1907.

The other plot showing an interesting continuity is the one
with the present address of No. 1 St Paul's Square. Today this

No. 1 St Paul's Square – a sixteenth-century timber-framed building encased in an eighteenth-century shell.

has all the appearance of an 18th century town house, but its façade conceals a virtually intact, jetted timber-framed building. The Priory Rental of 1507 refers to the building as The Falcon. A deed of 1705 refers to "the Ship, formerly the Seven Stars, formerly the Falcon". The Ship is listed in the Enclosure Award as occupying the same site as The Falcon.

A little alley known as Pudding Lane ran between the houses on the south side of the square from the poultry market down to the river. This ran alongside what is now the Magistrates Court. Writing of Pudding Lane in London, John Stow said it was so called "because the butchers of Eastcheap have their scalding house for hogs there and their puddings with other filth of beasts are voided down that way to their dung boats on the Thames". If Pudding Lane in Bedford had ever been used for a similar purpose, it must have been stopped by the regulations laid down in the Black Book of Bedford. Not only did these regulations instruct butchers to dispose of their offals in Offal Lane but it also specifically forbade them from throwing "any duste myer donge or carren or any other noysome thing into the Water of Owse" on pain of a forfeit "for every defaults to the chamber xxs".

The area on the eastern side of the High Street, opposite St Paul's Square, was dominated by the castle in the early Middle Ages, but after the castle had gone a row of houses had developed backing onto the boundary ditch of the castle. Some of these were accredited by the Rental of 1507 with prestigious tenants. The Swan Inn, for example, standing more or less on the site of the present Swan Hotel, was held by the Master of St Leonard's Hospital. This was the leper hospital which stood on the edge of the southern limit of the town. Sir Edmund Lucy and Lady Elizabeth Joye each had houses, one on either side of the little lane which marked the old entrance to the castle, now known as Castle Lane. During work on the new Wilkinson's Store in the late 20th century, archaeologists found the remains of a sizeable medieval hall. Sir Edmund was a member of the Lucy family based on Charlecote in Warwickshire. It is interesting that his messuage in the High Street included a tavern, indicating that, like the tenants of The Cury, he too had an interest in local catering.

The Stonehouse and Later Gaols

Gooseditch Lane, on the northern side of St Paul's Square, was also known as Stonehouse Lane. This was a reference to the Stone House which stood at its eastern end. This is marked on Speed's map as the Moot Hall. It was serving as the Moot Hall, or Guildhall, during the 16th century. That was where the Corporation of Bedford held their meetings. How long this had been the case is not known. It was certainly in existence in 1438 when it was the scene of rancorous confrontation between the followers of Lord Grey and those of Lord Fanhope which resulted in several casualties (see below).

The original function of the Stone House seems to have been as a gaol. In 1166, it was decreed that gaols were to be built in any town where they did not already exist. Pipe Rolls for the 12th century have several references to repairs to Bedford Gaol. The Pipe Rolls were the records of accounts of the office of sheriff. Those officials were in charge of the king's gaols and royal castles. So at that time Bedford Gaol was almost certainly within the castle complex. If so, it would have been demolished, along with the rest of the castle, following the siege of 1224. It is significant therefore that in 1225, the year after the siege, a special writ was issued ordering the Sheriff of Bedfordshire to "build a good strong gaol". This would have been the Stone House, which stood just across the High Street nearly opposite the former entrance to the castle. Although the castle itself no longer existed, the gaol was still referred to as "the gaol of Bedford Castle" for at least three centuries after that event.

In 1552, Sir Oliver St John, who was probably sheriff at that time, received a grant of 400 loads of stone from the late monastery of Warden towards the building of a new gaol. This was presumably the County Gaol at the corner of Silver Street. "Gaol Lane" was being used as an alternative name for Silver Street

in the early 17th century. This is the gaol where John Bunyan
was imprisoned from 1660 to 1672. In 1801, a new county gaol
was built in a different location more or less on the site of the
present H.M. Prison. The Silver Street prison continued to be
used, though, as a local lock-up for temporary detention as late
as 1831.

In addition to the county gaol, there was a town gaol, used
for offenders under the jurisdiction of the borough. This was
also housed in the Stone House in the early days but, in 1589, it
was deemed "both noisome to the town and to those committed
thereunto" and the gaol was moved to the old chapel which
stood on the bridge. This did not prove to be an ideal solution.
Throughout the 17th century, the corporation minutes indicate
that it was in constant need of extensive repairs. Thus, in 1661,
the bailiffs reported that "the Town Prison on the bridge is far out
of repair so that it is not fit to secure prisoners". The final blow
came in 1671 when, as a result of a great flood, "the stonehouse
called the Bridge House is totallee fallen down and the rest
much shaken and like to fall down". Even then it was agreed
that "the prison upon the Bridge shall be rebuilt". In the event,
however, as 18th century deeds show, the prison was rehoused,
for the time being, back in "the prison called the Stonehouse in
Stonehouse Lane". The Guildhall was still housed in the same
building at that time. This was the situation until 1806 when the
Improvement Commissioners ordered that buildings in Stone
House Lane be demolished as part of their programme to clear
ground in St Paul's Square for the erection of a new Guildhall.
The demolition programme included the Stone House itself.
The Corporation was temporarily accommodated in the Sessions
House which had been built in 1753 to house the Assizes. The
new guildhall was never built and the Corporation had to wait
until 1892 when what had been Harpur's School, on the south-

west corner of St Paul's Square, became the Town Hall. The town gaol was moved to a custom-built prison in St Loye's near to the new County Gaol. Eventually the two gaols were merged following Robert Peel's reform of the Penal Code in 1823.

The Chapel of Herne

In the south west corner of St Paul's Square stood a little chapel known as the Chapel of Herne or St Mary in Angulo. The name is descriptive of its position, "herne" meaning "corner" in Old English and "angulo" having the same meaning in Latin. The origin of the chapel is obscure. When it was being demolished in 1813, a local amateur archaeologist, Mr Charles Abbott, took the opportunity to carry out a little archaeology. He discovered a stone coffin lid bearing a symbol which he interpreted as a caduceus, the staff with intertwined serpents, usually associated with the pagan god Mercury. He described this as "a strange mixture of pagan and Catholic superstition" and on this basis surmised that it might be either a tomb of King Offa or of Archbishop Oskytel, both of whom were allegedly buried in Bedford. In fact, similar designs can be found on later coffins. One, for instance, at Bedford Museum, is from the site of Greyfriars Friary. They did not come to Bedford until 1238. Although he excavated to a depth of about four feet under the lid, he could find no evidence of a coffin or any bones. He did find, on the wall of the chapel, an inscription in some sort of antique lettering which he believed to be a reference to King Offa. However, Dr Martin Allen of the Fitzwilliam Museum, Cambridge, has transcribed the inscription to read " DA'G G YT DA".

He dates the inscription to "no earlier than the 13th century and no later than the 16th century", with nothing to connect it with King Offa. Mr Abbot's sketches of the inscription and of the coffin lid, together with letters he wrote to Mr Urban,

The inscription copied by Mr Charles Abbot from the wall of the Chapel of Herne.

editor of The Gentleman's Magazine, can be seen at the Bedford and Luton Archives and Record Services. The Gentleman's Magazine did not publish this correspondence. Drawings of the chapel itself show it to have been a small rectangular building with a window in the east wall in the Early English style of the 12th and 13th centuries. This dating is compatible with the earliest known documentary reference to the chapel. This is in a deed of Nicholas, Archdeacon of Bedford, dated "before 1180". Nicholas was a canon of St Paul's Bedford and also a prebendary of Lincoln Cathedral. In the deed he granted to the newly founded Newnham Priory the tithes of Hordehide, Bedford School and St Mary's Chapel, i.e. the Chapel of Herne, not to be confused with St Mary's Church. The school was, of course, the Priory School in School Street.

The chapel was in the possession of Lincoln Cathedral for most of its existence. By the 15th century, however, it had fallen out of use as a place of worship and was in the king's gift by reason of its being counted among the temporalities of the cathedral. During the Commonwealth period, all cathedral lands were invested in trustees for the use of the state and, in 1650, the chapel was sold to Bedford Corporation who intended to use it to house the Assize Courts. At the Restoration in 1660, ownership was returned to Lincoln Cathedral but it was leased to Bedford Corporation who used it for the Assize Courts and other public meetings. They also sub-let it to various tenants on the understanding that it should be available for public use and that "to that end upon warning (the tenant was) to remove his goods and lumbar out of the house and to white the walls and repair the floor of the house".

In 1753, a new Sessions House was built and the chapel was no longer required for public use. The Lysons brothers in the first edition of their book, published in 1806, reported that it was, at that time, being used as a brewery, under lease from the Dean and Chapter of Lincoln Cathedral. In a later edition, published in 1813, they included an addendum to the effect that the building was then unoccupied. During this period the building had also been in use as a storehouse by Joseph Barnard, the coal merchant and banker.

In 1813, the Harpur Trust purchased the building and demolished it to use the space for a playground for Bedford School which was then situated just to the north of the chapel in what was to become the Town Hall. It was at this time, during the demolition of the building, that Mr Abbott was able to make his discoveries. Just before the purchase and demolition, Thomas Fisher was able to make a drawing of the chapel. This was published among a collection of etchings in 1836, under the caption "A chapel which formerly stood in the Churchyard southwest of St Paul's Church". The drawing shows the chapel to be in a dilapidated state with the east window bricked up and the east wall itself supported by two buttresses, badly damaged at their lower ends. No doubt, they had suffered from the passage of heavy wagons when the building was being used by brewers and coal merchants.

The Chapel of Herne before it was demolished in the late nineteenth century.

St Paul's Church

As we have seen, St Paul's Church itself is probably the oldest religious foundation in Bedford, although its present appearance would not lead one to suppose that, especially if one compares it with the churches of St Peter de Merton and St Mary, where Saxon and Saxo-Norman fabric can be seen. Some Saxo-Norman work was revealed during 19th century restoration but the earliest surviving feature is the south door which has been dated to the Early English period of the 12th and 13th centuries. The main fabric of the church has been dated to the 14th and 15th centuries but it owes much of its present appearance to 19th century restoration work.

In 1996/7, during the conversion of office buildings on the north side of St Paul's Square to convert them into a new public house, evidence of an early cemetery was revealed. At least three separate phases of burial were identified. The burials were orientated east to west with the heads at the western end in the Christian tradition. The absence of grave goods and the presence of coffins make it unlikely that the cemetery pre-dates the middle Saxon period and the cemetery had apparently been abandoned by the 10th to 11th centuries. Further work is required to obtain more precise datings but already it is obvious that the cemetery was in use during the time of the Saxon burh and before the Norman occupation. Any further information will obviously have an important bearing on the history of St Paul's, and indeed, of Bedford town.

Other North to South Streets

On John Speed's map, the western half of the town is dominated by a street running north to south parallel to the High Street, corresponding to the modern Harpur Street. At that time the street terminated at its junction with Lime Street. The northern continuation was not constructed until the 19th century. This street fits in well with the rectilinear street pattern of the Saxon burh running, as it did, south from the northern boundary. On Speed's map it is called Sheps Chepping, meaning Sheep Market. The name dates back to, at least, the 15th century when it appeared in a deed of 1414 as Le Schepyschepping. This sheep market was conveniently situated just round the corner from Butcher Row. Speed's map shows a clear area the east side of the street which may have been the site of the sheep market. Today, the area is occupied by the Harper Suite and the Central Library.

There was an alternative name for this street which is much more significant with regard to the earlier history of Bedford. In the Newnham Priory Rental of 1507, the street is referred to as The Aldermanbury. Like its namesake in London, this can be taken to refer to the fortified homestead of Ethelred, Elderman of Mercia. Nothing remains of that homestead to indicate its location but there are early deeds which indicate the area where it was situated. Thirteenth century documents, for instance, refer to a "territory of Aldermanbury". Thus an item in the Harrold Cartulary dated 1240/50 refers to a messuage "of the fee of Aldermanbury", which lay between the "water called Severne and the messuage of John Hanslope". Another, dated 1260/70, refers to a messuage in "the territorium of Aldemannes beri", which abuts on one side of the way which leads from the cemetery of All Saints towards "Colleswell". The street now known as Allhallows was once known as Colles Lane and Speed's map shows a small symbol, indicative of a well in Well Street near the southern end of Colles Lane. Thus these two references place the "territory of Aldermanbury" in the north west quarter of the town.

Another indication is that this part of the town is virtually empty of property claimed by Newnham Priory in its Rental of 1507. This can be explained by the assumption that it was mostly held by the Abbess of Elstow. She had a strong connection with the Eldermanry of Bedford. The province of Mercia was organised into shires in 1008 during the reign of Ethelred the Unready. When Ethelred was replaced by the Danish king, Canute, the term Alderman began to be replaced by the term Earl. In 1016, Siward, one of Canute's supporters, became Earl of Northumberland and Huntingdon, which included Bedford. After Siward's death in 1055, the earldom passed to Tostig, brother to Harold who was later to become the last Saxon King of England. Tostig was found guilty of murdering two thanes and was outlawed by King Edward the Confessor and banished. The earldom passed to Harold. Tostig was eventually killed fighting his brother, now King Harold, at Stamford Bridge. Meanwhile the earldom of Northumberland and Huntingdon had been split. Northumberland was given to Morcar and Huntingdon, including Bedford, went to Waltheof who was married to Judith, niece to William of Normandy. William, of course, deposed Harold and assumed the crown of England in 1066. In 1076, Waltheof was found guilty of treason against William and was executed. The earldom passed to his wife Judith who founded Elstow Abbey. It was said that this was an act of contrition because it was she who had betrayed her husband to her uncle. Be that as it may, Judith's daughter married Malcolm of Scotland. Malcolm eventually inherited the Earldom of Huntingdon and Bedford and continued his mother-in-law's interest in Elstow by granting the Aldermanbury in Bedford to the Abbess. The grant included the "one third penny" rent due to Malcolm from Bedford, one of the perquisites due to an elderman of a burh. Thus it is possible to trace an unbroken line of succession with regard to "the territory of Aldermanbury" from Ethelred of Mercia to the Abbess of Elstow.

Apart from the absence of Newnham holdings in that part of

the town associated with the Aldermanbury, there is one positive piece of evidence to demonstrate that the Abbess of Elstow did hold property in that area. This is in a deed of 1513, concerning a property which once occupied a site on the western side of Harpur Street. For this particular property the deeds went back to before the Dissolution. It was described as "a tenement with a garden adjoining in a street called Shepyschepynge". The deed carried an endorsement to the effect that a free rent of 8d per annum was to be paid to the Abbess of Elstow. The site was a comparatively narrow strip of land, lying at right-angles to the street aligned with the old gate house in the messuage of the Old George, although, of course, there was a road and several buildings in between. This leads to the speculation that, at one time, the gatehouse was associated with the Aldermanbury itself.

The Angel Inn

One of the properties which came to be built between the Old George Gatehouse and the Abbess of Elstow's holding was an inn called The Angel. This, for a time, lent its name to the street which became Angel Street. The inn stood on the eastern side of the street. The earliest reference to the Angel Inn is in a marriage settlement of 1628, but there is reason to believe that the inn was much older than that. There is circumstantial evidence that there was some connection between the inn and the sheep market. That most famous of Angels, the one at Islington, stood adjacent to the rallying point for drovers before they ventured into London with their beasts. There was an Angel at Smithfield and one at Holborn where drovers kissed a pair of ram's horns, kept at the inn, as part of a ceremony giving them "freedom of the borough". We do not have to look further than St Luke's account of the first Christmas Eve to find a reason for connecting angels and sheep.

In the early part of the 18th century, the inn comprised a substantial building surrounded by a complex of outhouses including stables and a brewery. By the middle of the 18th century, though, it was no longer an inn. It is not listed in the innkeeper's recognisances of 1751 and, by 1760, part of it was being used as St Paul's Parish Workhouse. When John Wesley came to preach in Bedford in 1759, part of the ground floor of the building was being used as a pig sty. He gave a sermon in one of the upper rooms but complained, "We had a pretty large congregation but the stench from the swine under the room was scarce supportable". This did not put the Methodists off though and, in 1762, the building was given in trust to Wesley or "other persons as he shall appoint —— to preach God's Holy Word". By 1805 the building had been replaced by a custom built Methodist Chapel and this was, in turn, replaced by an enlarged chapel in 1832. This was eventually demolished in 1969 when the Central Library was built.

There is some indication that the plan of the Saxon burgh included another north to south street on the eastern side of the town. If so, this was at least partly erased when the Norman castle was built. This was roughly equidistant from the High Street as Harpur Street/Aldermanbury was on the western side. The eastern end of Castle Lane takes a turn to the north which brings it on the line of such a road. Speed's map shows a continuation of the road south into the castle precinct and property boundaries continue the line to the north. When the castle was built it would have effectively removed its function as a thoroughfare, so now only a short fragment remains.

Peck's Farm

Just to the east of St Cuthbert's Church, Speed's map shows a building which he calls Pieck Place. It appears on the map as a fairly large homestead with various outhouses. The immediate environs of the house, together with an orchard and garden, occupied the area now bounded by Newnham Street to the north and Castle Road to the south and extending along Newnham Street as far as the Castle public house. An indenture of 1477 indicated that William Peck and his son John let to the prior of Newnham "all their lands and tenements in the town and fields of Bedford, Goldington and Clapham. Those pertaining to Bedford amounted to about 72 acres. The Pecks did, however, retain for their own use "all the chambers both above and below at the western end of the hall —— with free entry and exit at suitable times, a principal stable for their horses and entrance to a garden on the north side of the hall to walk for their recreation". The indenture also excepted certain properties around the town including "The Cock" which stood in St Cuthbert's Street just north of the church and a tenement called Byshoppes which stood in Well Street. The prior was to hold the lands and properties outlined in the indenture for 8 years from Christmas 1477 for £8 down and £2 per annum. Eventually the prior acquired full title to all the property and, in a terrier of 1502, it is described as "land formerly of William Peck's".

William was MP for Bedford in 1449 and he had been JP for Bedfordshire for the years 1437 to 1440. This was a troubled period in English history. The young and unworldly Henry VI was on the throne, but real power was in the hands of the rival parties of York and Lancaster. The local representatives of those factions were Lord Fanhope of Ampthill for the Lancastrians and Lord Grey of Wrest for the Yorkists. William Peck was a supporter of Lord Fanhope. The rivalry of these magnates was fuelled by local issues and there was more than one occasion when armed bands of their supporters came into confrontation. Probably the worst of these occurred at Bedford Moot Hall in January 1439.

During a session there, a scuffle broke out between the rival supporters; the overcrowded staircase collapsed and 18 men were killed in the crush. The Patent Rolls report two enquiries into this affray. The first, dated March 7th 1439, lists a number of participants present. These included "William Pekke of Le Hoo late of Coupull". The second, dated May 30th of the same year, gave a further list of participants but this time William Pekke appears as one of three JPs who were asked to report on the event. During the proceedings it was alleged that "a multitude assembled from divers counties to the number of 800 or more (sic), for the most part girt with swords and uttered contumelious words in the presence of the said justices". However, despite this horrendous description, the conclusion was "that all are excused and that the said certificate was made of mere malice. This particular "Battle of Bedford" was not, it seems, of great importance to the forthcoming Wars of the Roses, but it was perhaps this brush with high politics that led to William Peck becoming MP for Bedford ten years later.

Some two centuries later a John Peck was Mayor of Bedford in 1694 and again in 1704. There is a memorial to him on the wall of St Paul's Church above the north entrance, so the Peck family seem to have been men of substance in the Bedford establishment over several centuries. On the other hand, in 1815, a Thomas Peck absconded for two days from the workhouse and, on his return, when he was refused supper, he struck the Master's wife, Sarah Davis, with a tin vessel.

Hassets

On the other side of the town, just to the west of Allhallows Street, Speed's map shows a substantial building laid out around three sides of a courtyard in the style of a Tudor Mansion. Speed does not name the mansion but it can be identified with one known as Hassets or Hassocks. This had probably replaced an earlier building on the same site because an entry in the Newnham Cartulary dated 1309, refers to "a former building space with courtyard enclosed with dykes, walls etc. "——" in Colles Lane in the Parish of St Paul's "——"and it shoots along the ditch called Saverne as far as the king's highway". At the time of the Newnham Priory rental of 1507, the house was occupied by Sir Edmund Lucy. He also had a messuage in the High Street next to the old entrance to the castle.

The Lucys were a Warwickshire family based on Charlecote Hall at Hampton Lucy. They acquired interests in Bedfordshire when Sir Thomas Lucy, who died in 1415, married Alice, the daughter of William Huggesford, who held manors in Wilden and Carlton. Edmund was the grandson of Sir Thomas. He had served under Henry VII at the Battle of Stoke in 1487, when the pretender, Lambert Simnel, was defeated. Edmund was knighted in 1502. His Ipm, dated 1506, confirms that he was seized of the manor of Wilden in Bedfordshire. It was his great-grandson, another Sir Thomas, who earned his place in popular history by prosecuting William Shakespeare for poaching deer on his estate at Charlecote, Shakespeare got his revenge by lampooning Sir Thomas in the character of Mr Justice Shallow who appears in the plays Henry IV part 2 and The Merry Wives of Windsor.

The house is listed as Hassets in the Hagable List of 1681 when it was ascribed to William Foster, the lawyer involved in the prosecution of John Bunyan. Foster was also assessed for nine hearths in the Hearth Tax return of 1671. This gives an indication of the size of the mansion. By the 18th century, the house was in decline and a deed of 1792 lists the names of various tradesmen occupying buildings "being near and formerly part of the mansion house called Hassets".

The Enclosure Award of 1796 allotted the property, which

it called Hassets, to Thurloe Brace Esq. who owned a total of some 9 acres of land in the area. Hassets is described as "a house, homestead, yard and garden". By the 19th century the property had been acquired by Alderman Thomas Gwyn Elgar who, in 1835, announced his intention of building upon the ground called Hassets. Now all that remains of this once great mansion is the name Hassett Street.

The Medieval Town South of the River

That part of the medieval town south of the river was much more precisely defined than was the northern part. Its bounds were definitively marked out by the King's Ditch. This ditch is clearly shown on maps of the town up to recent times, but it is now almost completely covered in, with only a few stretches still visible. A short length, for instance, can be seen running across the traffic roundabout at the southern end of St John's Street. Other fragments can be seen behind St John's Hospital and in the grounds of Dame Alice School. It originally formed a rough semicircle, with its western end leaving the River Ouse from the southern bank opposite Batt's Ford. From there it curved round to its southernmost point on St John's roundabout and then curved north again to rejoin the Ouse just below Duck Mill Weir. This most easterly point is marked by King's Ditch Bridge which carries the public footpath over the Ditch. The Ditch might have been intended as a defence and demarcation line but it also seems to have had an inhibiting effect on the development of this southern part of the town. All through the medieval period, and well into modern times, the built-up area has been confined within the Ditch and along only two thoroughfares. Of these, one was the continuation of the High Street. At one time this continuity was reflected in the name. The section south of the bridge was still called High Street. On Speed's map, that section down to St Mary's Church was labelled Bridge Street and it is not until well into the 18th century that the name St Mary's Street came into use. The southern section, beyond the St Mary's crossroads, was called St John's Street from at least the 15th century, and presumably acquired its name following the foundation of St John's Church and hospital in the 12th century.

The other thoroughfare ran east to west, intersecting the north to south street to form the cross roads by St Mary's. This comprised Cauldwell Street on the west and Potter Street (now Cardington Road) on the east. Cauldwell Street led, of course, to Caldwell Priory. Apart from the High Street, it is the only street in Bedford to have retained its original name, with only minor changes of spelling for all its known existence. Potter Street indicates that it was the site of a potter's or potters' workshops, and fragments of medieval pottery have been found in the area in some quantity. These two roads were two of the roads which originally converged on the river and were diverted onto the central cross roads when the southern town was laid out.

Apart from lanes leading to Duck Mill, which perforce was on the river, these two thoroughfares were the only two roads in the southern town until well into the nineteenth century and all buildings lay along those roads. Speed's map shows most of the buildings, in the conventional way as lines of terraces house, with two exceptions, one of these being a large house which stood at the bottom of St John's Street on its western side. The map shows this as a relatively big building, standing back from the road from it along a broad driveway. A building corresponding to this house also appears on Jefferies map of 1765 but by then it had lost some of its glory, as the approach way is shown to have buildings on either side. It was then called Rosemary Alley. By the time of Brayley's map of 1807, the driveway has been given the name Pepper Alley. There is no sign of the large house on

Reynold's map of 1841. The name was then still Pepper Alley but it was eventually given the name St John's Place. An early photograph shows it to have been occupied by a row of three storey artisans' houses. These were demolished in 1951 and the site was built over with modern development.

In the late 15th century, the large house had been occupied by Richard Kempston. The Kempston family had been prominent members of Bedford society for many years. William was Mayor of Bedford several times during the 14th century and was MP for Bedford in 1360. Roger Kempston was MP in 1382 and 1388. Thomas Kempston also served as MP and Mayor several times in the 15th century. He died in office as mayor in 1457. He was a close associate of Lord Fanhope of Ampthill. An entry for 1438 in the Calendar of Fine Rolls states that "the king has committed to the said John (i.e. Lord Fanhope); by mainprise of Thomas Kempston of Bedford, the keeping of all said castles, manors etc.". He was also present at the riot at Bedford Moot Hall in January 1439 when Lord Fanhope's supporters clashed with those of Lord Grey of Wrest.

The other place where Speed has used a non-conventional representation of houses is in the open square opposite St Mary's Church, which Speed's map shows to have been occupied by a scatter of four detached buildings. This had been the site of the third church in the southern town, St Peter's de Dunstable. The origins of this church are not clear. It presumably came under the patronage of Dunstable Priory, sometime in the 11th or 12th centuries. According to the Lysons, it had its own parish before the year 1400, but they give no evidence for this and there is nothing known of its geography. Certainly, by 1443, it was sharing a parish with St Mary's Church. The two churches were providing separate services with only one priest. This situation led to the near-farcical end of St Peter's about a century later.

It seems that services were held on alternate weeks in the two churches, with added complications when the dedicatory Saint's Days fell in the wrong week. Many items, including sacred vessels and books, had to be carried across the road from one church to the other as needed. Not surprisingly, this proved too much for one priest and he retreated to Buckinghamshire. The Bishop, left with two churches and no priest, finally persuaded him to return but only on the understanding that one of the churches be pulled down. St Peter's drew the short straw and was demolished. The fabric of the old church was used to good advantage. A large proportion of the stone was used to enlarge St Mary's Church; the south door went to the new free school and the north door to St Peter de Merton where it can now be seen as the south doorway. This has a dog-toothed semicircular arch, typical of the Norman period of architecture, so provides a clue to the latest period when the church might have been built. A window went to the so-called St Mary's Abbey, a large medieval house that stood in Cardington Road until 1968. Some of the coping stones were used to repair the parapet of the town bridge and the rubble was used to strengthen the metalling in various streets around the town. The font disappeared for three centuries, but it turned up in use as a horse-trough in the yard of the Angel Inn in Cauldwell Street. It can now be seen in the Archaeology Centre in St Mary's Church.

In 1554, the now vacant lot became the site of a market following a royal grant. The market was to be held on a Tuesday.

In 1760, the site was laid out as a handsome square, planted around with trees. This involved the demolition of certain old buildings belonging to the rectory of St Mary's. These included "an old market cross now entirely out of use, a blacksmith's forge, two small tenements, all of which said premises are in a very ruinous condition". These were, presumably, the buildings

The south door of St Peter de Merton Church – formerly part of St Peter de Dunstable.

represented on Speed's map. A pig market continued to be held in Potter Street, opposite St Mary's Church in the yard of the Fountain Inn.

Chapter 7

The Fields of Bedford

Most of the area now occupied by modern Bedford and its suburbs was open country in the Middle Ages. As was general at that time, this consisted of open fields cultivated in strips. These strips were held by individual farmers, but the strips belonging to any individual farmer were scattered in a more or less random manner over all the fields. It has been suggested that the object of this was to ensure that the early settlers would have had a fair share of good and poor land. The disadvantage of the system was that every man had to cultivate his land in step with his neighbours, following a timetable laid down by the manorial court. Thus everyone had to plant the same crop and harvest it at the same time as everyone else in a particular bundle of strips or furlongs. From early times, therefore, it must have been the ambition of every landowner to amass contiguous strips, so forming a block covering an area big enough to make it viable to throw a fence around it and form a close. He could then cultivate it as he pleased, regardless of the manorial regime.

In the early days, this enclosure movement was carried out by private treaty. Individual landholders would buy or exchange strips to collect sufficient land in one area to form a viable close; a sort of agricultural game of Monopoly. This activity reached a peak when, following the Tudor revolution, the power of local government was moving away from the manorial courts and being taken up by the parish councils. This led, in some cases, to quite large areas of a parish being enclosed in relatively small closes. In other areas, only a small proportion of a parish would be so enclosed and the remainder would continue to be cultivated on the open field system until the Parliamentary Enclosure Acts of the 18th and 19th centuries. Under these schemes, a whole parish was surveyed and the land was shared out in large enclosed fields between the principal landholders on a pro-rata basis according to the total holdings of each landholder.

It can be deduced which enclosure period gave rise to any particular field by the shape and size of the field. Early enclosures resulted in relatively small fields with sinuous boundary hedges reflecting the sinuous furrows made by the cumbersome ox-drawn ploughs. The Parliamentary Enclosure fields, on the other hand, were much larger and enclosed in straight boundaries mapped out on the drawing boards of the enclosure surveyors.

The make up of the boundary hedges also gives a clue as to the age of the enclosure. This has given rise to Hooper's Hypothesis of hedgerow dating. According to this hypothesis, the age of a hedgerow is proportional to the number of different shrub species which can be identified in a 30m to 50m stretch of the hedge. As a rough rule of thumb, each different species represents one century in the life of a hedge. The oldest hedges are those created by the Saxon settlers. They asserted into the native woodlands but left narrow strips of woodland to mark the boundary between them and their neighbours working from the other side. These hedges would therefore contain all the natural species of the wild wood and could easily include the 10 to 11 species required by Hooper's Hypothesis to take them back to Saxon settlement times. During the enclosures of the late Medieval period, new hedges were being planted, but the hedges would still be made from locally available shrubs, so hedges from that time would contain 3 or 4 species taking them back to the Tudor period. By the time of the Parliamentary Enclosures, hedge construction had become much more scientific and species were especially selected to make the hedges less penetrable by livestock. These new hedges would therefore consist of a single species, such as hawthorn, which would make a formidable barrier to cows and sheep and which could be easily plaished to maintain that barrier.

In the fields of Bedford, relatively few early enclosures took place and most of the fields remained open till the Parliamentary Enclosures, in 1795 in the fields north of the river and 1799 in the fields south of the river.

The Fields North of the River

One of the earliest recorded enclosures in Bedford was Sparrow Croft or Close. This is clearly marked on several maps and was situated on the western side of Kimbolton Road at its southern end. The enclosure can be traced back to a deed of 1329 by which Simon Collebar of Bedford granted to Hugh Sparwe (sic) and his wife Margaret, "8 selions of land lying together in the Field of Bedford in a furlong called Tokyes Hegges with the headland and balk adjoining between the lands of the said Simon and the Rector of the Church of St Peter de Merton and extending towards the south to the land of the said Simon". From another document we learn that the road to the east of Sparrow Close, i.e. the present Kimbolton Road, was at one time known as Cucking Stool Lane and must have marked the beginning of the route that the Cucking Stool took to carry miscreants down to their watery fate at Duck Mill (see below). But most of the early enclosures took place in two specific areas.

One of these was the Prebend Fields which lay between what is now Midland Road and The River Ouse. The name "Prebend" is from the same root as "provender" meaning "providing food". The produce from the Prebend Fields was used to maintain the canons of St Paul's Church when it was a collegiate church i.e.

before Newnham Priory was founded. Some of the canons were also prebendaries of St Mary's cathedral at Lincoln, and land at the western end of the area is ascribed to the prebend of St Mary's Lincoln in the Rental of Newnham Priory of 1507. The Rental shows that by that time the area had been completely enclosed into small properties. No doubt this had been facilitated by the fact that it was already under the control of one group of landholders.

The extent of enclosure is so complete that it has been possible to allocate all the properties mentioned in the Rental. All the area can be filled and this has been done in a diagrammatic map.

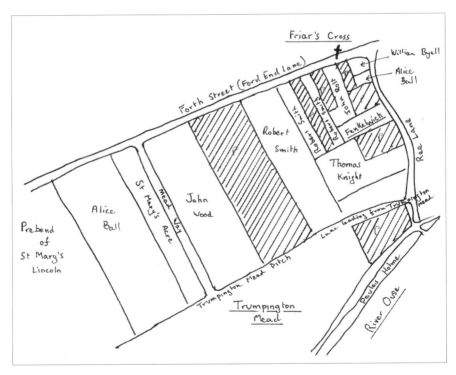

Diagramatic reconstruction of the Prebend Fields.

(Names are those of the people occupying the plots in 1507)

The larger closes, for which acreages were given in the Rental, have been drawn to scale but not necessarily to shape. The northern part of the area was occupied by a collection of small tofts and closes, none of them bigger than 5 acres. The southern part was occupied by a relatively large meadow of 20 acres known as Trumpington Mead. This bordered the river and so would have been exposed to frequent flooding. This would explain why it had not been taken into cultivation like the smaller closes to the north. A ditch, called Trumpington Mead Ditch, separated the meadow from the small closes and protected them from flooding. The meadow was approached by two lanes. The Mead Way provided access from Forth Street. This seems to have been approximately on the line of the present Prebend Street but it is difficult to be precise when comparing old documents with modern maps. Another lane "leading from Trumpington Mead" crossed the little stream which ran down to the Ouse along what is now River Street, via a ford known as Abel's Forth after Abel Attewater who at one time held land in the area. This ford was later known as Batt's Ford or Battison's Ford after a family of coal merchants who had wharfs along the river near that point, in the 18th century.

One or two other points can be expanded upon. The Friar's Cross stood in Forth Street at the southern end of an old pathway called Friar's Walk. The Walk was the path used by the Greyfriars to approach their preaching cross. This was later developed into a lane called Greyfriars' Walk and eventually became the wide and busy dual carriageway which it is today. One of the closes was called Fenkelwicke, meaning fennel wick, i.e. a plot where that flavoursome herb and vegetable was grown. Another close is a good example of an "extra-territorial" part of a parish, as it was not only occupied by the master of St John's Hospital but is listed as being in St John's Parish.

The other area of early enclosure lay on the eastern side of the town, in an area between the two Goldington Roads. (see above). At the time of the Newnham Priory Rental of 1507 these two roads were both referred to simply as Goldinton Way. One of the closes was known as "the Hernecroft". This is described as "lying between Goldington Way on either side and it abuts east on Goldington Way". This confusing entry is explained by placing "the Hernecroft" or "three-cornered field" in the corner formed at the point where the two Goldington Ways diverged, i.e. at the extreme eastern end of the between-roads area. Other closes, "Sexton Piece" and "Stoney Piece", can be precisely located because they appear on a sketch map accompanying a deed of 1773. On the basis of these three pieces, and taking into consideration the acreages given for them, the area between the two Goldington Ways can be mapped out.

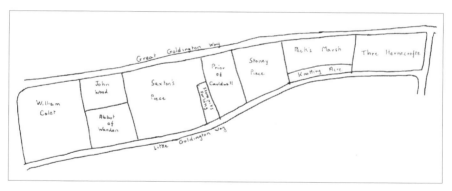

Diagramatic reconstruction of the closes lying between the two Goldington Roads (names are those of the people occupying the close in 1507).

The position and extent of the open fields north of the river is given on a pre-enclosure map of 1791. They formed an arc around the town separated from each other by the roads radiating outward from the town.

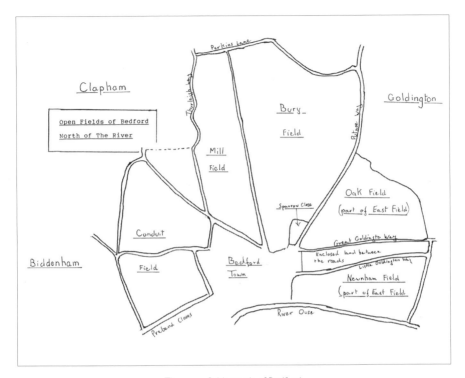

The open fields north of Bedford.

Conduit Field occupied the area between Forth Street and Clapham Road and bordered by Biddenham to the west. The Greyfriars were well known for constructing waterways or conduits across their land to serve their friary buildings. The friary buildings stood in Conduit Field, so such a waterway would explain the name.

Middle Field lay between Clapham Road and Clapham Park Way (now Foster Hill Road), with Clapham on the west and north.

Bury Field lay between Clapham Park Way, which was known as Little Berry Lane in the 18th century, and what is now Kimbolton Road, with Putnoe to the north. The name "Bury" or "Berry" shows a connection between the field and Bury Farm, whose 16th to 17th century farmhouse stood near St Peter's Church until it was demolished in the 1880s. The name has an intriguing archaeological ring to it but the reason is not known. F.W. Kuhlicke put forward the suggestion that the earliest "burh" was located in the area but there is little to support this except that St Peter's Church has Saxon work in its fabric and stands on a hill dominating the flood plain of the Ouse.

East Field, also known as Oak Field, lay between Kimbolton Road and the River Ouse, with Goldington to the east.

According to the Newnham Priory rental of 1507, the priory held about a quarter of the land in these open fields, mostly in Middle, Bury and East Field (alias Oak Field). (See table below). The smallness of the priory holdings in Conduit Field indicates that the Greyfriars were the dominant landholders in that area.

Name of Field	Total Area of Field (Acres)	Area Held by Newnham	% of Total Held by Newnham
Conduit	271	17.5	6.5
Middle	250	71.5	28.6
Bury	448	136.5	30.5
East/Oak	420	135.0	32.1
Total	1389	360.5	26.0

In the other fields, the Newnham holdings tend to be together in large blocks. Thus, in East Field the priory held Newnham Haylands containing 44 acres, while in Bury Field, Newnham held a large tract of land comprising 100 acres. This is described as "freshly cultivated" (terra frisce). Another two parcels of land in Middle Field, making together 9.5 acres, are similarly described. This implies that even at the end of the 15th century there was still land that had not felt the plough.

The 100 acres parcel in Bury Field are in about the right place, and the right size, to be the pre-cursor of Brickhill Farm. This farm survived as an agricultural unit until well into the 20th century. The land was built over to form the Brickhill Estate in the 1960s. The farmhouse stood near the site of the shops in Brickhill Drive. The pond which served the farm can still be seen in the patch of grass across the road from the shops.

A comparison of the pre-enclosure map of 1791 with a terrier of Brickhill Farm of about the same date enables some, more precise, localities to be identified. Thus, in Conduit Field, Yrenwell (Alias Ironwell) lay south of Bromham Road in what is now the Greyfriars area, and Green Ditch was the boundary ditch between Bedford and Biddenham. Middle Furlong (not Middle Field) occupied the middle of Conduit Field, as the name implies. Larkslade lay to the east of Thurleigh Way (see above), near the point where it began to form the boundary with Clapham.

It is tempting to identify Potage Acre in Bury Field with Plum Pudding Acre in the Brickhill terrier. The latter was situated in the area now occupied by the grounds of Bedford School.

It is also tempting to identify Putnoe Hedge with the Fuzzen Hedges mentioned in the Brickhill terrier. This ran roughly parallel to the present Kimbolton Road and about 50 m to the west of it. If so, they marked an early boundary with Putnoe over which Bedford had expanded at some later date.

It has been suggested that Hawkeswell was the precursor of the lake in Bedford Park, but there is no positive evidence to support that assumption. (See Appendix 1).

At the time of the pre-enclosure map of 1791, the East Field was clearly divided into Oak Field, to the north of the Goldington Highway, and Newnham Field, to the south. Early 16th century documents, however, make it clear that East Field and Oak Field were used interchangeably to cover the whole of the East Field. Thus "the Terrier of lands of the Prior and Convent of Newnham" lists several parcels of land scattered over East Field, and the same parcels of land can be found in "the Terrier of lands of the Priory" formerly "William Peck's" where they are listed in Oak Field. A possible explanation of the name Oak Field is given in an ancient undated deed, probably of the 13th century. This refers to land adjoining the road that led to Newnham Priory and is described as being "super quercum", i.e. above the Oak Tree. For it to be quoted in a deed, the oak tree must have been a well recognised landmark and had probably been used as a boundary marker, as oak trees frequently were. So it is quite likely that the tree gave its name to the field in which it stood. This deed, incidentally, is the one that led Farrar to mistakenly identify "the Old George" as the "prioratus" or town office of Newnham Priory (see above).

The area to the south of the Goldington Roads was also known as The Sele. This was further subdivided into Over Sele to the north and Nether Sele to the south, bordering on the River. Part of the Nether Sele included the Burgess Plots. They occupied a band of land running for about 700m to a width of about 200m, between what is now Shaftesbury Avenue and Rothsay Road, and including what is now Russell Park. These were parcels of land assigned to the Burgesses of Bedford. Among the privileges accorded to Bedford by Richard I in 1189 was the right to have a merchant guild. The members of the guild held exclusive rights of trading in the town, attended meetings of the Common Council and the Common Hall and could vote for the principal officers of the town such as the mayor. The guild consisted of two classes, freemen and burgesses. Admission to the burgess class was restricted to the eldest sons of the burgesses, making the burgess class hereditary, the principal distinction between burgesses and the freemen.

Under the Enclosure Act of 1797, the Burgess Plots were awarded to the 5th Duke of Bedford. In 1884, the 11th Duke gave 22 acres of that area back to Bedford, with the words "The Embankment has been brought under the able management of the Corporation to a state of great perfection, forming a most striking feature of the town and it would give me great pleasure to facilitate the future scheme of the Corporation for continuing the successful treatment of the embankment". The Duke's offer was gratefully accepted and after some discussion it was decided to lay the land out as a recreational park. There was also some discussion as to what to call the park. "Newnham Park" was favoured by some but "Russell Park" was eventually chosen as a compliment to the Duke. It was during the landscaping of the park that the warrior graves described above were discovered. Newspaper reports of the day (September 2nd 1898) describe how at the extreme eastern side were found antique capitals, broken columns and millstones – relics of Newnham Priory and its mill.

The Sele was crossed by several roads connecting Newnham Priory to Bedford Town. One of these ran along the north bank of the river through to what is now Newnham Avenue. This road was diverted away from the riverbank when Russell Park was laid out. Another road to Newnham, which ran across to the Priory from Peck's Farm, formed the dividing line between Over Sele and Nether Sele. Part of the road was still marked on the O.S. map of 1882 and the eastern part of it can be traced on the pre-enclosure map of 1791.

Writing in 1831, Matthiason described it as "a walk across the fields from castle Street (now Newnham Street) to the Priory ruins".

The area north of Goldington Road was known as the Haylands, subdivided into Newnham Haylands and Bedford Haylands. The 44 acres ascribed to the priory in the rental 1507 accounts for the section on the east, i.e. nearer to the Priory, leaving the area nearer to Bedford town as Bedford Haylands.

The Fields South of the River

This area was completely contained within the parish of St Mary, except for a small enclave belonging to St John's parish. The whole area covered some 640 acres. A survey carried out just before the Parliamentary enclosure of 1799 listed 102 old enclosures and homesteads, covering a total of some 140 acres.

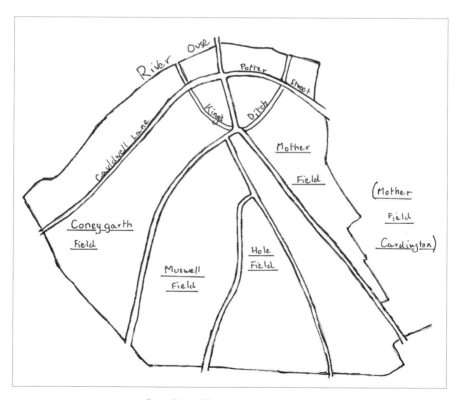

Open fields of Bedford, south of the river.

Most of these were in the Cauldwell Street vicinity. These covered a total of 105 acres, spread over 29 properties. In Potter Street, where 18 properties were listed, the total acreage was 18 acres. The remainder were small properties within the built-up area of the town, i.e. St Mary's Street and St John's Street. Very few of these covered more than an acre and were mostly described as "house and garden".

The remainder of the area was divided into four open fields, namely Coney Garth, Muswell, Hole and Mother Field. Coney Garth indicates a field where rabbits were found; Muswell suggests a mossy spring; Hole probably meant a secluded nook and Mother field implies a field assigned to a widow. These names can be recognised, albeit with slight variations in spelling, in earlier documents, but there are indications that there had been various changes of boundaries over the years. Mother Field, for instance, was adjacent to a field in Cardington also called Mother Field, and the two were separated by a very irregular boundary line suggesting that the original Mother Field was contained wholly in either Cardington or St Mary's Bedford. There are also indications of boundary changes involving Kempston. Joyce Godber, in her book "The Story of Bedford", makes the statement "an Augustinian priory was set up west of Bedford, that of Caldwell which was in Kempston Parish". Joyce Godber offers no evidence for locating the priory in Kempston and in later years it was known to be on the Bedford side of the Bedford/Kempston boundary, adjacent to its north eastern side to the King's Ditch, the semicircular ditch which separated the township of Bedford from its fields on the southern side. There is, however, support for Joyce Godber's statement from various documents which refer to "Barkes Ditch". This, according to Mawer and Stenton, "is commonly supposed to be the same as that known as King's Ditch". A deed of 1200/1201, for instance, tells us that Guy, son of Henry, quitclaimed to the Prior of Cauldwell, "land in Cameston, (i.e. Kempston) near Barkesdig", implying that at that time Kempston extended up to Barkesditch alias King's Ditch. An indenture of 1546 by which William and Ann Gostwick conveyed to Thomas Leigh the buildings and lands of Cauldwell Priory contains a list of the fields involved. Barkesditch is mentioned but not King's Ditch. In 1330, the prior of Cauldwell, among others, was brought before the Justices of the County of Bedford for having "stopped and levelled a certain ditch called Kyngesdych". Thus it would seem that the names "Barkesditch" and "King's Ditch" were indeed interchangeable and that Kempston did, at one time, extend up to that ditch and did include Cauldwell.

The more recent boundary between Bedford and Kempston followed a curve running parallel to the King's Ditch but some 1.5 kilometres from it. This line continued, forming the boundary between Bedford and Elstow, suggesting that Elstow, like Kempston, had surrendered its northern tip to Bedford at some time. The line stopped, however, at Cardington. This retained a tongue of territory extending up to the limit of Bedford Town. Cardington differed from Kempston and Elstow in that it was in Wixhamtree Hundred, whereas the other two were in Redbournestoke Hundred. The boundary between the old hundreds probably lay along the western side of Mother Field, putting that field wholly within Cardington. It is probable that the hundred boundary derived at this point from the Danelaw Boundary set up under the 9th century treaty between Alfred and the Danish leader Guthrum. This must have run somewhere through the land and countryside south of Bedford and, as a boundary of national importance, would have been respected by later hundred boundaries. Over the years, the Danelaw lost its significance; the hundreds themselves lost importance as local administration units in favour of the parishes, and the parishes would have undergone local adjustments such as we have seen between Bedford and Kempston, Elstow and Cardington. Other examples can be found between Elstow and Cardington which had contiguous fields called Sharp Field, and between Kempston and Elstow which shared Cow Meadow. Indeed, until relatively recently, this field was literally shared between the two parishes which had equal rights over it. The boundary across the meadow was not finally defined until the Kempston Enclosure Award of 1804.

Chapter 8

The River Ouse

The town of Bedford owes its very existence to the River Ouse. As the name implies, Bedford was a point at which the river could be forded and the town grew around that important crossing point. From earliest times, then, the river was of strategic importance. But it was also of economic importance as a source of energy to drive watermills and a source of food in the form of fish. It was also a route for the transport of heavy freight but that did not reach its peak until the 17th, 18th and 19th centuries.

The Bridge

At some point in time, Beda's Ford was replaced by a bridge. This must have been constructed at or very near the position of the ford because the approach roads to Bedford, from both north and south, are aligned on the bridge.

The first bridge would almost certainly have been made of wood and might go back to Mercian times, as the triple obligation, that required every man to support the defence force, help maintain fortresses and maintain bridges, was established at the time of King Offa. Haslam has put forward an hypothesis that the town of Bedford was established as part of a defence strategy of Offa's but there is no concrete evidence to support this. We can presume, though, that there was a bridge by the time that Edward the Elder caused a burh to be constructed, south of the river, in 916. There was definitely a bridge by the later 12th century and this must have been built of stone as there was a chapel on it by that time. This chapel was the subject of a grant by Simon de

Beauchamp to the Hospital of St John at Bedford. It could be the association with St John's Hospital that led the Lysons brothers to describe the chapel on the bridge as "a free chapel or oratory with a hospital".

By the 14th century, the chapel was in the charge of a chaplain or warden appointed by the townsmen of Bedford to celebrate divine service. He had the power to collect tolls that, together with rents from certain properties in the town, were to be used for maintenance of the chapel and of the bridge. These sources of revenue were evidently insufficient as, in 1342, the warden was given protection for proctors sent "throughout the realm to collect alms for the fabric of the chapel". The chapel stood near the centre of the bridge and there was a gatehouse towards the southern end. About this time, the sheriff, acting on behalf of the King, challenged the townsmen of Bedford over their right to appoint the chaplain, and submitted a nominee of his own. This created a dispute that lasted for some twenty years, during which time the bridge and the chapel were suffering from neglect with no one actively responsible for their upkeep. The townsmen petitioned parliament with the request for a speedy resolution of the dispute. The wording of the petition has caused some confusion among later historians. It describes the chapel as being "over the water on land belonging to Lord Mowbray and adjoining the bridge". Some writers have interpreted this as meaning that the chapel in question was on the bank of the river and not the one on the bridge. Hassal and Baker, following a suggestion by R. Gilmore, show a chapel on the south bank of the river, more or less on the site of the modern Moat House Hotel, but this could not be correct as Lord Mowbray possessed no land south of the river. The paradox is resolved by examination of some 18th century illustrations of the bridge. These show the chapel standing on the little island which also supported the

Detail of an eighteenth century print showing how the chapel "on the bridge"
was "semi-detached" from the bridge itself.

central pier of the bridge, and abutting against the bridge like
one half of a semi-detached house. At some stage an archway or
gatehouse was built from the chapel across the bridge.

The dispute between the sheriff and the townsmen was
eventually resolved; the chaplain was made answerable to the King
but the townsmen were granted pontage, i.e. the right to charge a
toll for the use of the bridge in order to pay for its maintenance.

Even under this arrangement new funds were needed. In 1451, Thomas Chalton, one time occupier of "The Old George", felt the need to include an item in his will bequeathing "40s towards the making of a new chapel at the foot of Bedford Bridge" and "5 marks towards the reparation of the said bridge". His example was followed by several others who made similar bequests, all referring to the "chapel on the bridge". These included John Stowe alias Bowes and William Joye who was a prominent landowner. The chapel must have fallen out of use by the middle or the 16th century as there is no mention of it in the Chantry Certificates of Edward VI's reign. Presumably it was out of line with post-Reformation ideas of what a chapel was for. In 1589, it took on a new function when the town gaol was transferred there from the Stonehouse (see above). The other structure on the bridge, the southern gatehouse, was, according to Henman, being used at one time as a magazine and storehouse for the County Militia.

With the coming of the stagecoach era, these structures were proving a hindrance to road traffic. They were removed and the parapet reconstructed in 1765. The bridge was still a hindrance to traffic, however, and the narrow arches supporting the bridge also hindered the flow of water, giving rise to flooding. In 1809, John Wing, the architect, presented a report on the state of the bridge to the Improvement Commission. In 1811, work was started on demolition of the old bridge and, by 1813, the new bridge was declared open to the public. The new bridge was essentially as it appears today, except that it was doubled in width in 1938/40 to cope with modern traffic. If one takes the footpath under the bridge from the east side of the High Street to the west side one can see, over one's head, the join between Wing's original bridge and the 20th century widening. This gives a clear idea of the width of Wing's bridge.

Water Mills

There were four water mills in the environs of Bedford during the medieval period; Newnham Mill, Joel's Mill, Port Mill and Castle Mill.

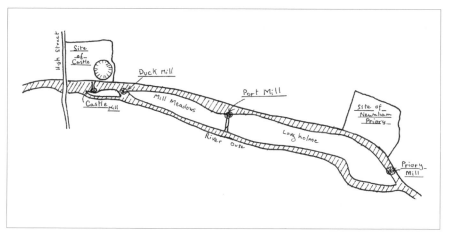

Bedford's water mills.

Duck Mill and Newnham Priory Mill survived till comparatively recent times so their positions are known.

The positions of Castle Mill and Port Mill have been deduced from various sources of information.

Newnham Mill was the one attached to Newnham Priory and was situated at the eastern end of the northern reach of the river, just before it rejoins the main river.

Joel's Mill is the earliest recorded mill and survived as a working mill, under the name Duck Mill, until the end of the 19th century. The earliest known reference to it is in a charter of Miles de Beauchamp granting the mill to the Abbot of Bermondsey. This means that the mill was in existence during the first half of the 12th century, i.e. before the establishment of Newnham Priory. The mill remained the property of Bermondsey Abbey till the Dissolution, but it was let out to various tenants including the Knights Templar, Fawkes de Breaute and Newnham Priory.

The indenture defining the letting to Newnham Priory, dated 1394/5, makes it clear that this mill was known as Gelysmulne at that time, and variations on that name, e.g. Joel's mill, Johelis Mill etc., continued to be used till the turn of the 16th to 17th centuries. Speed's map of 1610 shows it as Duck Mill, but an entry in the Newnham Priory Rental of 1507 makes it clear that this was on the site of Joel's Mill. The name "Duck Mill" needs some explanation. Very few water mills are without ducks, so the name can hardly have been intended to refer to those birds. The name is more likely to have arisen from the use that was made of the mill pond around that time. John Bunyan was baptised by total immersion there; witches were "swum" there and it was probably the place where miscreants were ducked after being paraded through the town on the ducking stool. The ducking stool was a form of punishment going back to, at least, the 11th century. The Domesday Book for Cheshire lays down "anyone who made bad beer was either put in the dung stool (a.k.a. cuckstool) or paid 4s to the reeves". Scalds or brawling women were also subjected to this punishment in some places. In the early days, the miscreant was made to ride in a tumbril or dung cart and paraded through the town, exposed to the scorn and abuse of their neighbours. It was a sort of mobile pillory. It was not until later that the "cucking stool" became a "ducking stool" and the shameful ride through the town terminated in immersion in water. This development seems to have occurred around the time that Joel's Mill came to be called Duck Mill. Mill ponds were convenient places for ducking. An old mill in Derby, for instance, was known as Cuckstool Mill, while the remains of a ducking stool were found in Vineyard in Winchcombe which was at one time known as Duck Street. The Abbess of Elstow had a cucking stool and she was arraigned at court in 1330 because "she has not punished offenders against assize of bread and beer by sentence of the cucking stool but has taken fines to the amount of 4s 6d". The mill was still working until 1891 when it was demolished to improve the amenities on the river and to better control flooding. The site is marked, and the name preserved, in Duck Mill Bridge.

The site of Port Mill is not so well documented but its position can be deduced from information from various sources. A charter of William de Beauchamp, dated 1220–60, included the grant of a fishery to Newnham Priory. This fishery is described in the Newnham Rental of 1507 as "a separate water" of the Ouse running from "Porte Mill to a great stone lying for a boundary between the said water and the water formerly Reginald Bray's, by the enclosed ditch of Bedford Castle". Similar limits are laid down in a document of 1515 by which Newnham granted, to the Mayor and Corporation of Bedford, a strip of common land "from a stone rock lying against Gebons Forth to the north flood gates where Port Mill stood". In width, the land covered the area from the said floodgates to Knyghtys Cross. The 'stone rock' is obviously the "great stone" mentioned in the Newnham Priory Rental. This would make Gebon's Forth the "old ford" marked on the map in Matthiason's "Bedford and its Environs", crossing the eastern part of the Castle Ditch, just before it entered the river. Knyghtys Cross is probably the "Kings Cross" mentioned by Leland in his "Itinerary". Leland tells us that the bones of many men were buried there. These would have included the bones unearthed when Russell Park was being laid out (see above). The cross was erected, no doubt, to mark the graves. All these clues come together if we assume that the "separate water" mentioned in the Newnham Rental was that limb of the river which runs north of Mill Meadows and Longholme Island, and that the strip of common land granted to the Mayor and Corporation of Bedford was along the edge of the Burgess Plots at the southern edge of what is now Russell Park. This strip of land corresponds to that tongue of Goldington parish which lay along the river until Goldington was merged with Bedford.

It is interesting that the "separate water" is what most modern Bedfordians would regard as "The River", but various alterations to sluices and weirs have radically altered its character. Port Mill would have been somewhere along this "separate water" and the most likely site for it would have been at Boatside Weir, near the Schools' Rowing Club boat shed.

The author of an article in Lock Gate argued that Port Mill Was a late name for Castle Mill, the last mention of Castle Mill being in 1330 about the time when Port Mill begins to feature in the records. However, it is unlikely that a mill, some 600m down stream from the castle, should be named after it. A charter of Simon de Beauchamp, dated before 1180, conceded "my mill known as Bedford Castle Mills" to Newnham Priory at an annual rent of 45s 4d in eels. Simon's son, William, confirmed this concession in the same charter in which he granted the fishery to Newnham. As mentioned above, the western limit of the fishery is defined in the Newnham Priory Rental as being "the water formerly Reginald Bray's by the enclosed ditch of Bedford Castle". In 1483, Reginald Bray had acquired that part of the Barony of Bedford that included the castle site. In the 14th century when the property belonged to the Mowbrays, it included, as well as the castle site proper, "an island called Faukes Herber and a fishery and no other property in Bedford". This fishery would therefore have been that bounding the western end of Newnham Priory's fishery, and the island called Faukes Herber would have been the little island called Swan Island in more recent years. Cary Elwes suggested that there was a barbican on this island, being a southern entrance to the castle via a causeway across the river. He linked this with an entry in the Pipe Rolls of 1187/8, "The sheriff had expended — in the works of the bridge of the

Castle of Bedford and of the postern towards the water £4 6s by the King's writ. Several authors have referred to the causeway but only one, G Hurst, in a paper presented to the BAAS in 1851, has left precise information about its position based on his own observation. "Part of the foundation of this wall (i.e. the causeway) can now be seen (in 1851) at low water". He placed the start of the causeway at the mid point of the river frontage of the castle. This corresponds to the position of a water gate, or postern, revealed by archaeological excavation on the site of the old County Library Building. Cary Elwes' theory about a southern entrance to the castle cannot be ruled out but it seems strategically unlikely, and it is more likely that the island which marked the termination of the causeway was in fact the site of the Castle Mill. This would be exactly analogous to the situation at Warwick Castle where the mill is at the end of a similar structure jutting into the River Avon.

Appendix I

"A Perfect Terrier and Survey of the Brickiln Farm" (c. 1750) (also known as Brickhill Farm)

1.   The Three acre piece against Nomans (?) Close abutting East on the leys belonging to the estate, the land belonging to the Berry Farm in John Sugar's occupation West, Nomans Close South and the Highway leading to the House North.

2.   Spring Acre, abutting North East on the House and South West on Mr Haw's land in Thos. Field's occupation, the land belonging to the estate on both sides.

3.   Dove House Piece, containing eleven and a half acres abutting North East on the Dove House Rickyard(?) and South West on Hill Highway and bound on both sides by the land belonging to the Estate.

4.   The ten acre piece, abutting South on Dove House Piece and North on Lodge Hole (?), two eight acres pieces belonging to the Estate East and Hill Highway West.

5.   The eight acre piece, against Jarvis' Gate abutting South to the eight acre piece that shoots to the Rickyard and North on Jarvis Gate, the five acre piece East and the ten acre piece West.

6.   The Rickyard Piece and (?) acres abutting South East to the Rickyard and North West on the ten acre piece, the Dove House Piece South West and the five and eight acre pieces on the North East. The five acre piece abutting South East on the Pithles and West on the eight acre piece against Jarvis' Gate. The Rickyard Piece South West and Clapham Closes, (viz) of Fuzzen Close North East.

7.   Jackmans Hill Piece by estimation 16 acres lies East from the House abutting North against Jackmans Closes and bounded on the South by Jackmans Hill Slade South East by the two acre

piece and North by the Pithle belonging to the estate.

8.   The two acre piece abutting as the last piece the Berry Farm Land in J. Sugar's occupation South East.

9.   Knolls Corner, two acres abutting South East on the Highway and North West on the land of the Rt. Hon. Earl of Ashburnham in Mr Willis' occupation, the land of Wm. Gerey Esq. in Thos. Eastwick's occupation on the South West and the Berry Farm land in J. Sugar's occupation North East.

10. New Close Acre abutting East on New Close and West on the land of The Earl of Ashburnham in Mr Willis' occupation South and the Berry Farm Land in J. Sugar's occupation North East.

11. Eight roods abutting East on the Berry Farm Land in J. Sugar's occupation(viz) against the Fuzzen Hedges and West on the land belonging to the Estate, the land of Lord Ashburnham in the occupation of Mr Willis on both sides.

12. ----------three lands, one acre East and West on Ozier Balk the land of the Earl of Ashburnham in Mr Willis occupation on both sides.

13. Same furlong two half acres abutting East on the Joint and West as before, the land of Wm Gery Esq in Thos. Eastwick's occupation South and the Berry Farm land in J. Sugar's occupation North.

14. Same furlong, three lands one acre abutting as before the land of Wm Gerey Esq. in Thos. Eastwick's occupation on both sides.

15. Same furlong, two half acre abutting as before on the land of Mr Haws in Thos. Field's and South on the land of the Earl of Ashburnham in Mr Willis' occupation North.

16. Plum pudding Acre, three lands abutting South on the Berry farm land in J. Sugar's occupation East and the Earl of Ashburnham in Mr Willis' occupation West.

17.   Round Acre, two lands abutting East on Mr Haws' land in Thos. Field's occupation and West on the land of Wm Gery Esq. in Thos. Eastwick's occupation (viz) the Gore Piece. The land of the Rt. Hon. Earl of Ashburnham in Mr Willis' occupation on both sides.

18.   Windmill acre, two lands abutting East on the Windmill and West on Mr Haws' land in Thos. Fields occupation and Mr Haws' land in Thos. Field's occupation North and the Rt. Hon. Earl of Ashburnham's land in Mr Willis' occupation South.

19.   The two acre piece by Berry Close side abutting East on Putney Road and West on the land belonging to the Berry Farm in J. Sugar's occupation. Berry Close South and the land of Lord Ashburnham in Mr Willis occupation North.

20.   Four lands one acre abutting on Berry Balk South and North on Mr Haws' land in Thos. Field's occupation and the land of Mr Haws' in Thos. Field's occupation on both sides.

Hill Field

21.   The nine acre piece on the Hill, the land of William Gery Esq. in Thos. Eastwick's occupation and the land of Lord Ashburnham in Mr Willis' occupation South, Lord Ashburnham's land in Mr Willis' occupation North, Hill Highway East and Waterthrorow Piece West.

22.   Waterthorow piece containing six acres abutting South to the Forty Roods and North to the land of Lord Ashburnham in Mr Willis' occupation and the Berry Farm Lane in J. Sugar's occupation North, the nine acre piece East and the twelve acre piece on the North.

23.   Twelve acre piece abutting South as before and Clapham Close West. The watherthorow piece East and abutting North on Lord Ashburnham's land in Mr Willis' occupation and Mr Haws land in Thos. Field's occupation.

24. The three acre piece against Perkins Lanes End, the land of Mr Benson in Henry Sharp's occupation South, Clapham Close Balk North, Wm. Gery Esq. Land in Thos. Eastwick's East and Clapham Close West.

25. Ten acre piece against Clapham Close Gate abutting East on lark slade piece and West on Thurleigh Highway Joint, the land of Mr Haws in the occupation of Thos. Field South and the twelve acre piece north.

26. Lark Slade piece containing twelve acres goes through two furlongs abuts South on Warden piece and North on the twelve acre piece, Mr Haws land in Thos. Field's occupation and Lord Ashburnham's land in Mr Willis' on the east of the upper furlong, Mr Haws land in Thos. Fields occupation east on the lower furlong, Thurleigh Highway on the upper furlong and the land of Wm Gerey Esq. in Thos. Eastwick's occupation west on the lower furlong.

27. Warden piece four acres abutting South on Mr Haws land in Thos. Field's occupation North on Lark Slade Piece and Mr Haws land in Thos. Field's occupation and the land of Wm. Gerey Esq. in Thos. Eastwick's occupation on both sides.

28. The five acre piece next Thurleigh Highway abutting South on Wm. Gerey Esq. land in Thos. Eastwick's occupation and Lord Ashburnham's in Mr Willis' occupation and North on the two acre piece, and the land belonging to the Berry Farm in J. Sugar's occupation West and Thurleigh Highway on the East.

29. The Two Acre Piece abutting East to Thurleigh Highway and West on the Frier's land in Mr Willis' occupation. The five acres South and Lord Ashburnham's land in Mr Willis' occupation North.

30. Tire devil Piece six butting South to the Berry Farm land in J. Sugar's occupation and North on the Road and Clapham Close Hedge, the land of Lord Ashburnham in Mr Willis' occupation

East and Mr Haw's land in Thos. Field's occupation West.

31. Hanging Piece three acres abutting South on the Kettering Road and North on Mr Haws' land in Thos. Field's occupation and the land of Mr Barker in Mr Franklin's occupation East and the Road West.

32. Three Acre Piece abutting South on Alone Willows Leys and North on Berry Farm land in J. Sugar's occupation and the land of Wm. Gery Esq. in Thos. Eastwick's occupation East and the land of Mr Haw's in Thos. Field's occupation West.

33. Two Acre Piece against the side of the hill abutting South on the land belonging to the Estate the land of his Grace the Most Noble John Duke of Bedford in Bennit's occupation and the land of his Grace in Henry Sharp's occupation North and Wm. Gerey Esq. land in Thos. Eastwick's occupation on both sides.

34. Two acre piece in Middle Furlong abutting South on the land of Lord Ashburnham in Mr Willis' occupation and North on the Estate, the land of Wm. Gerey Esq. in Thos. Eastwick's occupation east and the land of the Corporation in occupation of Bennit West.

35. Lower Furlong two acres abutting on South on Berry Balk and North on Wm. Gerey's land in Thos. Eastwick's occupation Mr Gerey's land in Eastwick's occupation East and Lord Ashburnham's in Mr Willis' occupation on the West.

36. Same furlong two roods abutting South as before and North on land belonging to the Estate. The land of the Friers farm in Mr Willis' occupation on both sides.

37. Same furlong two roods more abutting South as before and North on the land of the Corporation in Thos. Bennit's occupation East and Mr Haws' land in Thos. Field's occupation West.

38. Same furlong four acres abutting South on berry Balk and North on the land of the ———— in occupation of John Bennit

and the land of Mr Haws' in Thos. Field's occupation on both sides.

Conduit Field

39. The three acre piece abutting South on the Provender and North on a Joint, the land of Mr Haws' in Thos. Field's occupation East and the land of Lord Ashburnham in Mr Willis' occupation West.

40. Ironwell piece by estimation two acres abutting South on the last furlong and North on the road leading to Olney, the land of Lord Ashburnham in Mr Willis' occupation East and the land of Wm. Gerey in Thos. Eastwick's occupation West.

41. The Waypost Acre four lands abutting South on Devil's Acre and North on a headland belonging to the Berry Farm in J. Sugar's occupation, the land of Mr Haws' in Thos. Fields occupation East and the land belonging to the berry farm in the occupation of J. Sugar West.

42. Conduit Piece three acres four thorow shot lands and one short land the Newport Road South and the Joint North, the land of Wm. Gerey Esq in Thos. Eastwick's occupation East and the Berry Farm land in J. Sugar's West.

43. Middle Field piece twelve lands containing three acres two of which abut longer than the rest southward on the land of Mr Haws in Thos. Field's occupation and the ten lands abutting South on Lord Ashburnham land in Mr Willis' occupation and North on a piece belonging to the Estate, the land of the Corporation in Thos. Bennit's occupation East and the land of Wm Gerey in Thos. Eastwick's occupation West.

44. Three lands at the upper end of Middle Field Furlong containing one acre abutting East and West Middlefield Furlong South and Lord Ashburnham's land in Mr Willis' occupation on the North.

45. Middle of the field two half acre lands abutting east on Lord Ashburnham's land in Mr Willis' occupation Mr Haws' land in Thos. Field's occupation South and Wm Gerey's Esq in Thos. Eastwick's occupation North.

46. Four lands one acre west of the three acre piece. The land of Wm Gerey Esq in Thos. Eastwick's occupation on the East and West.

47. Gallows Piece nine gores containing three acres abutting South on the Road and North on Green Ditch, the land of Mr Haws in Thos. Field's occupation on both sides.

48. Seven lands containing two acres abutting West on a headland belonging to the estate three lands South of Green Ditch, the land of Mr Haws in Thos. Field's occupation on both sides.

49. One land and Gore by Bedingham Balk with the hedge and ditch containing one acre abutting South on Mr Gerey's land in Thos. Eastwick's occupation and Lord Ashburnham's land in Mr Willis' occupation East.

50. Claycroft Corner eleven lands with the hedge and ditch containing two acres, the berry farm land in J. Sugar's occupation South and Claycroft Lane North.

51. Tenn (sic) lands containing four acres abutting East and West and bounded on the north by lord Ashburnham's land in Mr Willis' occupation and the land of Wm. Gerey Esq. in Thos. Eastwick's occupation on the south side.

52. The two acre piece against the Kettering Road abutting South on Lord Ashburnham's land in Mr Willis' occupation East and land of Mr Haws in Thos. Field's occupation West.

53. John Bush piece six lands containing two acres abutting South on land belonging to the Berry Farm in J. Sugar's occupation and North on the Kettering Road, the Berry Farm land in J. Sugar's occupation South and Lord Ashburnham's land in Mr Willis' occupation North.

Newnham and Oak Fields

54. Penny piece containing six acres abutting South on the River furlong and North on Little Goldington Way, the land of Richard Lane West, and the land of Mr Haws in Thos. Field's occupation East.

55. Same furlong abutting as before, two lands, one acre, the land of Wm. Gerey Esq. In Thos Eastwick's occupation West and Lord Ashburnham's land in Mr Willis' occupation. East.

56. The four acre piece, the lands abutting South on River Furlong Joint and North on Little Goldington Way, the Land of Wm. Gerey Esq. in Thos. Eastwick's occupation on both sides.

57. Windmill (sic) Piece in River Furlong abutting South on Mills Leys and the River and North on Haggets Piece. Mill Lays East and the Corporation land west.

58. Between the roads, three lands one acre abutting South on Little Goldington Way, and North on Great Goldington. Way, the land of Wm. Gerey Esq in Thos. Eastwick's occupation East and the Lord Ashburnham's land in Mr Willis' occupation West.

Oak Field

59. Middle Furlong four lands one acre abutting East on Lord Ashburnham's land in Mr Willis' occupation and West on Mr Gerey's land and bounded on the North by Gerey's Esq. land in Thos. Eastwick's occupation. A footpath balk on the East.

60. Three lands one acre in the bottom Furlong abutting east to the forty acre piece belonging to the Lord Ashburnham in Mr Willis' occupation and West on Middle Furlong the land of Mr Haws in Thos. Field's occupation South and Lord Ashburnham's land in Mr Willis' occupation on the North.

61. Claypit Piece, four acres part of which goes through two furlongs, six lands at the East end and five at the West end, the land of lord Ashburnham in Mr Willis' occupation South and

the land of the Berry Farm in John Sugar's occupation on the North.

Appendix 2

Bedford's Street Names

Many of the names of the streets of central Bedford were first recorded in the Middle Ages, some as early as the 13th century. These developed as a result of common usage and have changed over the centuries, in some cases many times. A more systematic way of choosing names was introduced in the mid-19th century, under the authority of the Improvement Commission. This Commission was set up in 1803, initially to supervise the rebuilding of the town bridge and the tidying up of the St Paul's Square area. It gradually expanded its authority to cover the whole town, with responsibility to decide when the streets were in good enough condition to be adopted for public maintenance and also to assign official names to the streets.

Some of the early street names are outlined below. The streets are listed under their modern names arranged in alphabetical order.

Allhallows

This street is first mentioned in 1260–70 in the Harrold Cartulary (BHRS XVII) as "the way that leads from the graveyard of All Hallows towards Coleswelle". This well was situated at the southern end of the lane in what is now Midland Road. The lane is referred to as Colles Lane, in 1309, in the Cartulary of Newnham Priory, (BHRS XLIII). The name Allhallows Street was used by Speed on his map of 1610 but Allhallows (Lane) has been used since. For a brief period in the 19th century, it was also referred to as Dines' Lane after a Mr Dines who had premises on the corner at its southern end. The lane had to be widened in 1836 to allow the passage of carts. It was then recommended for adoption by the Improvement Commission who had finally chosen the name Allhallows Lane in 1835.

Cardington Road

The road was referred to in the Newnham Priory Cartulary, (c.1300) as Potter Street. There is evidence for pottery activity in the street during the Medieval Period. "Potter Street" continued in use till the 1870s but Kelly's Directory of 1885 used "Cardington Road".

Castle Lane

This lane has always been associated with the Castle and there is some evidence its outlet onto the High Street might have marked the position of a barbican. The Rental of Newnham Priory (1507) refers to it as "a lane leading to Bedford Castle", and Speed used "Castle Lane" on his map of 1610.

Cauldwell Street

This name has been used, with minor variations of spelling, since it first appeared as a street name "Cauldwelle Street" in a deed dated to 1270–1310. It is named after the priory which was founded in the 12th century and was known at that time as Caldwell Priory. On his map of 1610, John Speed uses Caldwell Street although that may be a misprint for Cauldwell Street. The modern form was officially adopted in 1807. The name means literally "cold well" and probably refers to a feature near the site of the Priory.

Duck Mill Lane

The Newnham Priory Rental of 1507 refers to this simply as Mill Lane but places it in St Mary's Parish. This clearly distinguishes it from the present Mill Street which is in St Paul's Parish. There are references to Milnelane in the 14th century but these do not specify the location.

The Improvement Commission chose Duck Mill Lane in 1835 but they were also using Bouy and Oar Lane in the 1840s after a public house of that named frequented by boatmen.

Dame Alice Street

A lane in this position is mentioned under the name Marston's Lane in a quitclaim dated 1559. From the late 16th to the 18th centuries it was called Bendhouse Lane, indicating that the area was involved in the tanning trade. Cole's map (1807) has it as Harpur Street (q.v.) but it was finally officially named as Dame Alice Street by the Improvement Commission in 1835 when they decided to use the name Harpur Street for the street which now bears that name. Dame Alice was, of course, the wife of Sir William Harpur and it was appropriate to maintain the Harpur connection as the Harpur Trust had been largely responsible for building the almshouses which replaced a number of cottages destroyed in a fire in 1802.

Foster Hill Road

This was referred to as Clapham Park Way in the Newnham Priory Rental of 1507. At that time it extended up to Clapham Park but the northern end now only survives as footpaths. It underwent several changes of name during the 18th and 19th centuries – Little Berry Lane (Jeffrey's map of 1765), Waterloo Road (Reynold's map of 1841), Cemetery Road (Improvement Commission 1856) but Kelly's Directory of 1890 listed it as Foster Hill Road. The Foster family farmed at Brick Hill Farm.

Ford End Road

In the 13th century (Newnham Priory Cartulary) this was "Forthe

Strete". It linked the centre of Bedford to the hamlet of Forth or
Ford End in Biddenham. The hamlet is mentioned in a charter
of William II. In the 19th century at least part of it was called
Cox's Pits Road after a stone pit which is marked on Bryant's
map of 1826. At one time it started from a point much nearer to
the centre of Bedford but it has gradually retreated as Midland
Road has advanced.

Gravel Lane

Now serving only as an access road to the rear of shops in Midland
Road, it was a lane called Ocles Lane at the time of the Newnham
Priory Rental (1507). Robert de Okele was a burgess of Bedford
and was assessed for a tannery in the Taxation list of 1297. John
and Thomas Okele were listed as burgesses in 1399.
"Gravel Lane" was used on Jeffery's' map of 1765, probably a
reference to a gravel pit in that area.

Horne Lane

The cartulary of Newnham Priory has this as Calteslane in the
early 14th century and "Calts Lane" was used by Speed on his
map of 1610. John Calt, who was living at the turn of the 13th
to 14th centuries, held land at the western end of this lane.
"Horne Lane" was used in the Bedford Corporation Minutes
of 1649 (BHRS 26) and the name was officially adopted by the
Improvement Commission in 1835. There is archaeological
evidence for the manufacture of small objects from goats' horns
in the area. Jeffery's' map of 1765 called it King's Lane but that
is the only instance of the use of that name and it was probably a
misinterpretation of a phrase such as the King's Highway.

Harpur Street

The southern end of this street was the site of a sheep market, le Schepyschepping in 1414 (BLARS X67/56). It is Sheps Chepping on Speed's map of 1610. The northern end was known as Duck Lane. e.g. Doke Lane in 1422 (BHRS 2) and Duck Lane on Speed's map. But the Newnham Priory rental of 1507 used a name which reflects a much earlier period of Bedford's history i.e. Aldermanbury, which takes it back to the Saxon period. In the 18th century, public house names were used for relevant parts of the street, e.g. Angel Street, after the inn which stood on the site of the present Central Library and White Horse Lane after a public house which stood on the present site of Marks and Spencer. In 1835, the Improvement Commission chose to name the whole length of the street, from St. Paul's Square to Dame Alice Street, "Harpur Street", introducing "Dame Alice Street for the street which had up till then been called "Harpur Street".

Kimbolton Road

The southern end of this road was known, interchangeably, as Cucking Stool Lane (i.e. the place where the Cucking Stool was housed) and Okelane (after the adjacent "Oak Field"). Both names were used in the Newnham Priory Rental of 1507. Kimbolton Road was introduced by the Improvement Commission in 1859, some sixty years after the road had been turnpiked all the way through to Kimbolton.

Lime Street

A mortgage of 1676 refers to this as Lime Kiln Lane or Gee's Lane. (BLARS X199/24). Jeffery's map of 1765 shows it as "Queen's Head or Duck Lane", while a feoffment of 1805 refers to "Lime Kiln Lane alias Queen's Head Lane". The Improvement

Commission chose Queen's Head Lane in 1835 but Kelly's Directory of 1885 has it listed as Lime Street.

Lurke Street

This was called Lorclaine in a deed of 1447, (BLARS X67/63) and the name has persisted with minor variations of spelling throughout its life. The modern form Lurke Street was used in Kelly's Directory in 1885. The significance of the name is obscure.

Midland Road

The Cartulary of Newnham Priory (1240) refers to this as Well Street after Colles Well which was sited in the road. (see Allhallows above).

The name was still in use in the census return of 1861 but by 1871 the name had been changed to Midland Road. The railway had come to that part of Bedford in 1859.

Mill Street

A deed of 1341 names this as Horsemylne (BLARS X67/39). Mill Lane was used, interchangeably, with School Street during the 15th to 17th centuries; e.g. a mortgage of 1447 has Scolestret (BLARS X67/63) while the Hagable Rental of 1681 has "Mill Street alias School Lane". The Improvement Commission settled for Mill Street in 1835.

Newnham Road

The Victoria County History of Bedford (vol 3, p8) has a 16th century reference to Temesse Street. This name, in the form Thames Street, was used throughout the 18th and 19th centuries. The name suggests that, in earlier times, the River Ouse was also known, at least in part, as the River Thames/(cf Mawr and

Stenton's discussion of Tempsford in "Place Names of Beds. and Hunts.". "Newnham Road" appears on the O.S. map of 1884. At that time the name included the continuation of the road along the Embankment.

River Street

The names used for this road have always reflected an association with a water course, e.g. Ree Lane in 1507 ("Ree" being a stream, channel or river), Water Lane during the 18th and 19th centuries and finally River Street, used in the 1871 Census return, for instance. It almost certainly indicates a small tributary, (later culverted), which ran down the line of the street to join the River Ouse rather than a lane leading down to the river itself.

Silver Street

The first recorded use of this name in Bedford is on Speed's map of 1610, but the name appears so frequently in other towns of Saxon origin that it is almost certainly older than that. Throughout the 17th and early 18th centuries, the name was used interchangeably with Gaol Lane (the gaol at one time stood on the corner of the High Street) e.g. "Little Silver Street alias Gaol Lane" appears in a will in 1653. The Improvement Commission used Gaol Lane in 1808 and 1815 but finally settled for Silver Street in 1835.

Tavistock Street

A deed of 1559 (BLARS X55/2) calls this Godestoklane. This might have been because it led to St Peter's Graveyard (i.e. God's enclosure) but there are records of a Wm. Godestoke in the early 15th century. (BLARS X67/50–53). It was known as Offal Lane during the medieval period, i.e. the place where the butchers of the town disposed of their less attractive by-products. When that end of the town became the site of fashionable expansion in the early 19th century, like the area, the name was gentrified and changed to Offa Street for a short time, but this was finally changed to Tavistock Street by the Improvement Commission in 1835, as a compliment to the Marquis of Tavistock, the courtesy title of the heir to the Dukedom of Bedford.

Index

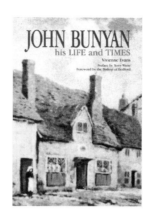

JOHN BUNYAN
His Life and Times

Vivienne Evans

Born to a humble family in the parish of Elstow near Bedford, John Bunyan (1628–1688) became one of the world's most widely read Christian writers – The Pilgrim's Progress eventually being translated into over two hundred languages.

This lively book traces the events of his life with its spiritual turmoil and long imprisonment, as well as discussing many of his writings. Clearly seeing Bunyan as a product of his time and place, it also explains the intriguing social, political and religious background of the turbulent seventeenth century.

THREADS OF TIME

Shela Porter

A pale-faced city child is evacuated from London during the Zeppelin raids of 1917. In Hitchin she takes a dressmaking apprenticeship and opens her own workshop with customers including the local gentry and the young Flora Robson.

Moving to Bedford on her marriage, her sewing skills help her rapidly growing family to survive the Depression; working long hours during the exigencies of war-time Britain, it is her re-designed battle-jacket that Glenn Miller is wearing when he disappears over the Channel in 1944, and entertainers Bing Crosby and Bob Hope leave comics and candy for her 'cute kids'. For five years after the war the family run a small café in the town but sewing then sees her through again as the business is sold, she is widowed with a nine-year-old son to raise, all her children gradually leave and she moves away to be wardrobe mistress to a big operatic society in High Wycombe. Finally she settles in a small cottage opposite the great airship sheds at Cardington from where she once watched the ill-fated R101 take off on its last journey in 1930.

A mirror of her times, this gripping biography tells the story of a remarkable lady, a talented dressmaker, mostly in Hitchin and Bedford – played out against the unfolding drama of the entire twentieth century.

JOURNEYS INTO BEDFORDSHIRE

Anthony Mackay

This book of ink drawings reveals an intriguing historic heritage and captures the spirit of England's rural heartland, ranging widely over cottages and stately homes, over bridges, churches and mills, over sandy woods, chalk downs and watery river valleys.

Every corner of Bedfordshire has been explored in the search for material, and, although the choice of subjects is essentially a personal one, the resulting collection represents a unique record of the environment today.

The notes and maps, which accompany the drawings, lend depth to the books, and will assist others on their own journeys around the counties.

Anthony Mackay's pen-and-ink drawings are of outstanding quality. An architectural graduate, he is equally at home depicting landscapes and buildings. The medium he uses is better able to show both depth and detail than any photograph.

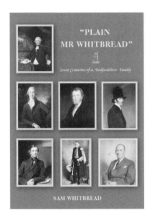

"PLAIN MR WHITBREAD"
Seven Centuries of a Bedfordshire Family

Sam Whitbread

The Whitbread family have been a part of Bedfordshire life since at least the 13th Century (and probably earlier). From small beginnings as peasant farmers, through appointments as local officials to the founder of the Brewery, one of the most notable success stories of the Industrial Revolution, and his son, the radical Whig politician and follower of Fox, the Whitbreads have gradually made their presence felt, first locally and later nationally. Six Whitbreads sat in the House of Commons for a total of 128 years, while at the same time building roads, bridges and hospitals, improving cottages and the local churches, and serving as magistrates, High Sheriffs and Lord-Lieutenants of the County.

The book's title is taken from the fact that at least two members of the family were offered peerages but preferred to "remain plain Mr Whitbread".

The author originally conceived the book as a simplified family history for his children and grandchildren but it will also appeal to those interested in the local history of Bedfordshire.

The narrative ends with the death of the author's father in 1985, but the author has added a "postscript" outlining the first seventy years of his own life.

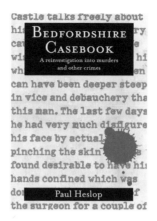

Castle talks freely about
hi... BEDFORDSHIRE ...ry
ca... CASEBOOK ...e
wi... A reinvestigation into murders ...hi
wh... and other crimes ...en
can have been deeper steep
in vice and debauchery tha
this man. The last few days
he had very much disfigure
his face by actual
pinching the skin
found desirable to have hi
hands confined which was
do...   Paul Heslop   f
the surgeon for a couple of

BEDFORDSHIRE CASEBOOK
A reinvestigation into murders and other crimes

Paul Heslop

This is a book about crime and punishment in Bedfordshire. It focuses mainly on the time when perpetrators were hanged for murder and lesser crimes, or sentenced to hard labour, or transported abroad for what today would be regarded as minor offences.

They range from the 17th century incarceration of John Bunyan, whose 'crime' was to preach outwith the established church; to rape and terror perpetrated by the man they called The Fox, on the South Bedfordshire borders in the 1980s. 'Domestic violence' features: the brutal murder of his wife by Joseph Castle in Luton in 1859, and the murder of 23-year-old Ruby Annie Keen at Leighton Buzzard by Leslie George Stone in 1937. We have the murder of Old Sally Marshall, at Little Staughton, in 1870; a Luton mugging that ended up as murder when William Worsley, convicted on the evidence of an accomplice, was hanged; and the A6 murder at Deadman's Hill, the infamous Hanratty case, still topical today.

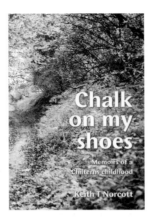

CHALK ON MY SHOES
Memoirs of a Chilterns Childhood

Keith T Norcott

Here is an affectionate remembrance of growing up in the 1930s and 1940s in the villages of rural Bedfordshire and the gentle hills of the North Chilterns, where Bedfordshire and Hertfordshire meet. We are taken back to villages like Lower Stondon and Stopsley and towns like Hitchin and Bedford when life was slower and simpler than it is today. Here too are descriptions of customs and practices that no longer exist, like the "penny picture" shows in the village hall, the local policeman who dishes out summary justice and the Queen of the May celebrations. And central to it all is the guiding hand and indomitable spirit of "Our Mum", who guided the family most of the time, and saw it through the horrors of the war.

Full of stories, anecdotes and impressions of the hills and communities of the area, this is a book to trigger memories in those who know this part of the country, and excite curiosity in those who are coming to it for the first time. The intervening years have seen great changes, but the hills still retain much of the charm they had in bygone days, a charm that is reflected in these pages.

CHANGES IN OUR LANDSCAPE:
Aspects of Bedfordshire, Buckinghamshire and the Chilterns 1947–1992

Eric Meadows

In the post-war years, this once quiet rural backwater between Oxford and Cambridge has undergone growth and change – and the expert camera of Eric Meadows has captured it all . . .

An enormous variety of landscape, natural and man-made, from yesteryear and today – open downs and rolling farmland, woods and commons, ancient earthworks, lakes and moats, vanished elms. Quarries, nature reserves and landscape gardens. Many building styles – churches of all periods, stately homes and town dwellings, rural pubs, gatehouses and bridges. Secluded villages contrast their timeless lifestyle with the bustle of modern developing towns and their industries.

Distilled from a huge collection of 25,000 photographs, this book oVers the author's personal selection of over 350 that best display the area's most attractive features and its notable changes over 50 years. The author's detailed captions and notes complete a valuable local history. The original hardback edition was in print for only 4 weeks in 1992. By popular demand now in a large format paperback.

BEDFORDSHIRE'S YESTERYEARS
Volume 4
War Times & Civil Matters

Brenda Fraser-Newstead

Social history comes to life, first-hand and vivid, when seen through the eyes of those who experienced and shaped it.

The 'Bedfordshire's Yesteryears' series contains many privileged glimpses of a way of life that has changed radically. Here is the generation of two World Wars; here are the witnesses to countless technological and sociological transformations.

This volume highlights the angst of the Depression and the two World Wars, when the whole social fabric was disrupted but showed extraordinary resilience. It also traces another major feature of the twentieth century, namely the rapid development in all modes of transport – carriers and trams, airships and fire-engines, trains and automobiles.

Route marches, the General Strike, the Home Guard, the munitions factory, the Land Army, barrage balloons, evacuees, G.I. brides, the Specials, steam fire-engines, double-decker trams, the concert party – just a few of the evocative words that roll away the decades.